In the Wake of the Giant

SUNY Series in the Anthropology of Work
June C. Nash, editor

In the Wake of the Giant

*Multinational Restructuring and
Uneven Development in a
New England Community*

Max H. Kirsch

STATE UNIVERSITY OF NEW YORK PRESS

Published by
State University of New York Press, Albany

For information, address State University of New York Press,
State University Plaza, Albany, N.Y., 12246

Production by Cathleen Collins
Marketing by Patrick Durocher

Library of Congress Cataloging in Publication Data

Kirsch, Max, 1953–
    In the wake of the giant : multinational restructuring and uneven
development in a New England community / Max Kirsch.
        p.   cm. — (SUNY series in the anthropology of work)
    Includes bibliographical references and index.
    ISBN 0-7914-3827-9 (hardcover : alk. paper). — ISBN 0-7914-3828-7
(pbk. : alk. paper)
    1. Pittsfield (Mass.)—Economic conditions.   2. General Electric
Company.   3. Downsizing of corporations—Social aspects—
Massachusetts—Pittsfield.   4. Industries—Social aspects—
Massachusetts—Pittsfield.   5. Pittsfield (Mass.)—Social
conditions.   6. Community development—Massachusetts—Pittsfield.
I. Title.   II. Series.
HC108.P72K57   1998
    330.9744′1—dc21   97-30362
                                                                                      CIP

10 9 8 7 6 5 4 3 2 1

Contents

Tables

Acknowledgments

This book would not have been conceived or completed without the guidance and inspiration of June Nash, who convinced me to pursue fieldwork in the United States and who provided the groundwork, generosity, and tolerance that saw this work completed.

More debt is due to varied sources, not the least from the memories of my father's lectures predicting the coming depression that was an inevitable result of the capitalist mode of production. Although that depression didn't occur in his lifetime, I now find myself making the same predictions, even if the scope has now widened from the United States to the entire world system. Inspiration also comes from memories of his work in a Borg-Warner plant that disemployed him shortly before he reached the required number of service years for a pension—moving production out of the area to sunnier climates. Cleveland, Ohio, as I was growing up there, was "deindustrializing"—the steel and other plants representing basic industry were closing up shop and leaving vast areas of the downtown region empty and depressed. While the city now claims to be in the midst of a comeback, it will never reach the heights of industry that made the robber barons wealthy and the city the home of some of the richest cultural institutions in America today.

My beginnings in anthropology were nurtured by Eleanor Leacock. "Happy" and her family provided more than a supportive niche for me throughout most of my career, grounding me when necessary and integrating me into the anthropological sphere as well as her house in the country and her loft in New York. I am only sorry that she did not live to see the completion of this work, which is dedicated to her memory.

My colleagues at the City University of New York's Central Office and the Graduate Faculty of the New School for Social Research were supportive of this work and tolerant of its production. Mary Rothein, Leon Goldstein, and Madleine Adler visited me in the field, providing support and encouragement.

I owe a debt that I cannot repay to June Nash and her family, who included me as one of their own. Laura Nash and Matthew McCaslin spent a fall season up in Massachusetts, entertaining me and providing a distraction to the work underway. Herbert Menzel, up until his untimely death, welcomed me and supported my presence. June Nash will doubtless recognize the intellectual debt to her in this work, which was conceived as a companion volume to her *From Tank Town to High Tech (SUNY, 1989)*. She is obviously not responsible for its shortcomings.

Eric Wolf, Edward Hansen, and Shepard Forman read the dissertation that led to this book, supporting me and providing useful comments. I am grateful for their input and their encouragement. Richard Feldstein encouraged the production of the book, recommending the manuscript to SUNY Press. Teresa Brennan read, pushed and encouraged me to get the book finished, providing invaluable insight. Finally, I am grateful for the support of the many friends who have helped me along the way. I particularly want to note Robert Gatto, Chris Stamp, Calixte Stamp, Susana Meyer, and Patricia Cooper.

The research was made financially possible by funding from the National Science Foundation and the National Endowment for the Humanities awarded to June Nash as principal investigator, which she generously shared with me, and from an award from the Wenner Gren Foundation for Anthropological Research. I am grateful to these institutions for their support and their confidence in a topic somewhat outside the traditional anthropological realm.

My family has witnessed all of the stages and pitfalls of higher education in a capitalist society. To them I owe a debt of perspective and a hope for the future that we share.

Introduction

American social and economic life is based on the community. Despite the recent trend to reify the importance of the family and family values, they do not exist without the communities by which they are reinforced and maintained. The community is the basis of identification for all individuals, and whether accepted or rejected, it forms the structure for everyday life and the fuel for our culture.

Communities have come under pressure by unstable economic forces and the deterioration of the social net. Wider economic and social forces, integrated into the global whole, have seriously affected the mechanisms by which communities operate and attempt to maintain recognized sets of rules and understandings. How they succeed or fail in maintaining continuity in the face of destructive forces is one of the important social questions of our time.

The largest threat to a community is changes in the way individuals and families are able to secure the daily necessities of living. Disruptions in work and industry are challenges to stability. The reaction a community has to change, whether internally produced or subject to forces beyond immediate control, can determine the survival or destruction of the social structure.

As theorists and commentators note, most of the world is subject to economic systems that are not based on the needs of individuals or their communities. Our present economic priorities are propelled by principles that further the desires of a few, not the majority who make the system possible. Ultimately, of course, this results in tension and conflict among those who manage the means of system profitability and those who work for them. This power imbalance and the differences in the rewards of labor it produces are the basis of economic unrest, but they are also the root of the social ills that are now part of the late twentieth century. The debates over our medical practices, the rise in crime, and the crises in education and housing are part of what a recent panel of anthropologists called the "Disorder of Industrial

Societies," all linked to the way in which we distribute available resources.[1] The destruction of the community and the social net it reinforces is the major disease of our time and one that the social sciences are only beginning to engage as a primary subject.

The social net has deteriorated on a national scale. Patients who can no longer afford to recover in hospitals are exiled to the streets; the ability to work is no longer a right but a privilege, and those who do so often find their wages incapable of sustaining a reasonable lifestyle. Even welfare, that ambivalent provision of government aid that at least provided food for those in serious trouble, is under attack.

What are the consequences of these transformations in the American lifestyle? The quality of life has deteriorated. Those who lived through the 1950s and 1960s saw endless possibilities of increasing social security and futures for their children. As Katherine Newman notes, the plant shutdowns of the 1970s and 1980s led to economic instability, one consequence of which is the downward mobility of children. Minorities in urban areas are the most seriously effected (Newman, 1994:131). But even in areas where outright poverty is not the most glaring effect, communities have undergone changes that reflect the priorities of American economics. The paternalistic firms of the late nineteenth century replaced some of the more "traditional" roles played by the patriarchal father figure in American families (Ewen, 1977). While the idea of the employer as protector and provider still exists, the symbol that stands as the Prudential Rock is now modified by the realization that this company regularly deceived its customers and employees. The rise of multinationals and other fiercely competitive firms have replaced the picture of the family-oriented company with one of bottom-line profit and "stockholder responsibility." This change in management orientation has eroded the basis for employer involvement in community life, and in some cases, of communities themselves.

Economic change necessarily implies cultural change. But while the relationship of industrial firms to communities has clearly been reoriented during the twentieth century, the cultural changes that follow are not always immediately apparent. The relationship between community and industry may alter before the perception of that change becomes clear. The community's unconscious—those perceptions of reality based on the experiences of the past—may be rooted in a vision of the community no longer in sync with corporate planning. June Nash has noted that often what was adaptive behavior in the past no longer serves to appropriately deal with current problems (1970:1). In the same way that Malinowski referred to "cultural survivals," Marshall Sahlins (1985:16) argues that "the past is not dead— because it is not past. The radical distinction that we make between diachrony and synchrony is in symbolic activity an indissoluble synthesis."

Still, these shifts have led to changes in the way that people react to their circumstances and view their lives. Finding jobs that will pay the rent or mortgage and also buy food has become a national preoccupation. Millions are forced into jobs that barely get them transportation to work. Most do not provide health insurance or other benefits. In 1984, there were more people toiling at McDonalds than there were people working in the steel industry in the United States (Davis, 1984).

What are the consequences? Many feel apathetic, hopeless to effect change. One need only to look at the voter participation in elections to know that a shrug and "What can we do?" are prominent statements. How is one to react when, while trying to put food on the table, a television news program informs us that GE chairman Jack Welch's compensation was over $30 million in 1996?

Americans, like their counterparts over the globe, are dependent on employers for economic security. The enclosure movement in England is the symbol of the change from land-based labor to the selling of wages as a commodity, the separation of the individual from life-practice. Communities are also dependent on these wages for their infrastructures and their networks. States are dependent on these communities for their income. What has resulted is the alienation of the worker from work, a separation integral to capitalist production that has many consequences both economically and psychologically. Nash, in her study of a Bolivian tin mining community, points to the three sources of alienation that Marx analyzed in capitalist production:

> 1) [The] separation of the producers from the product, or the alienation of surplus value; 2) separation of the producers from the means of production, which forces them to become dependent on the owners of capital to make a living; and 3) separation of the producers from the source of meaningful self-involvement in the work process. (1979:325)

To this Nash adds a fourth component, "the separation of the workers from the sense of identity with a community" (Nash, 1979:325).

There is resistance, though, active and passive. There has been a long and involved history of union activity in the United States, one that has been actively fought by the owners of capitalist enterprises. These struggles have won the entitlements that Americans have enjoyed, such as Social Security, health care, a rising standard of living, and education for their children. It is these rights that are under increasing attack as industries claim competitive disadvantages. The recent rise of union activity provides hope for those who have experienced the decline of active unionism, sent into decline by economic forces stronger than perceived abilities to confront them.

The other side of this resistance is passive. Workplace absenteeism is at an all-time high. Individuals no longer feel loyalty or an obligation to function adequately at their jobs. There is also a rise in self-destructive behavior—wars fought over religious righteousness, racism, blaming victims for psychological shortcomings, crime, family deterioration, and depressive apathy. While these are often viewed as character flaws, and are used for ideological purposes as explanations of the American state, they are also acts of resistance to circumstances seemingly beyond individual control.

Global cities, as Yago (1983:115) tells us, are internationally rather than nationally oriented, interfering with stable economic growth in local areas. The strategies of multinationals ignore the needs of communities in favor of competitive advantages in the global marketplace. Development is not planned "as if neighborhoods mattered" (Schwartz, 1981:64). While community leaders may realize that strong neighborhoods are needed to prevent crime and provide welfare for its members, corporations are concerned only with the provision of a labor force necessary to effectuate their accumulation of capital.

Many inner cities now resemble Third World areas. Residents are left to provide for themselves without employment opportunities or adequate housing, food, or even sanitation facilities. The social disease to which the authors of *Diagnosing America* refer is growing as citizens are not allowed to participate in the structuring of their lives.

This book results from research in Pittsfield, Massachusetts, a town in western New England. Undergoing economic restructuring—alternately referred to as "deindustrialization" or "downsizing," depending on the period—the organization of the social structure is being transformed. The town has similarities to many towns and cities across the United States and indeed, around the globe.

While I do not claim that this locality represents a community as *sample* (see Arensberg, 1961), it does possess parallels that make comparison to other communities possible. Many regions are now reacting to rapid changes that are beyond direct local control. The evolution of the community in Pittsfield is unique to the population that lives there, but such processes of change have taken place in cities and towns across the country. Barry Bluestone and Bennett Harrison have called this process "deindustrialization"—manifested in the loss of industrial jobs and the consequent lower-paid service opportunities that sometimes become available. This circumstance is now referred to as "downsizing" or that action that corporations take to reduce the number of their employees. As we shall see later, this reduction is selective.

As in this New England town, the multinational organization of business is often at odds with local interests and produces incompatible explanations of benefit and need. These contradictions are based on the interest of the concerned parties and are cloaked in ideologies that attempt to explain to various audiences what has happened and why it has occurred.[2] Because communities are not homogeneous entities, the presentations of these ideologies differ within the community as well as outside of it.

Communities confront the hybrid of growing social problems and the hope of new development. Based in part on magical thinking, communities hope that they can attract enough new industry to counter the destructive economic impact of industrial movement and capital flight. What often holds communities back, as we are frequently told, are the resources that the community is willing to contribute to the effort. This criticism equates problems of development with those of "attitude," the community's seeming unwillingness to get off their collective behind and pull themselves up by their bootstraps. A convenient explanation of why development is not working, the argument neglects to discuss the *distribution* of resources. Those with resources, most often those in power, figuratively or literally, do not willingly give them up. Those without them are blamed.

Pittsfield is no exception. It has based most of its economic hope on the attraction of new industry and the stabilization of its current economic resource, General Electric. Unlike many other communities in the United States, however, Pittsfield has never before had to chart its own path. Its history since the beginning of the twentieth century is analogous to that of a mining town. Despite other small industries, it has been completely dependent on the corporation for its direction. General Electric has run Pittsfield. Managers move around the country often, ostensibly to learn the businesses, but effectively functioning to keep them separate from the communities in which they live. Its "nonnatives" rarely become true residents. Decisions are made either by managers based in Fairfield, Connecticut, where the corporate headquarters is, or locally by temporary personnel. Pittsfield's development efforts and economic restructuring have always been accomplished from the outside.

It should not be surprising, then, that most hope for development has focused on the attraction of outside industry and the hiring of outside consultants. "Native" points of view have rarely been taken seriously, even by residents.

Berton Berry (1973) has delineated four styles of urban planning that include

> 1. Ameliorative Problem Solving, or "the natural tendency to do nothing until problems arise or undesirable dysfunctions are perceived to exist in sufficient amounts to demand corrective or ameliorative action";

2. Allocative Trend Modifying, which he calls "future-oriented versions of reactive problem solving";

3. Exploitative Opportunity Seeking, where an "analysis is performed not to identify future problems, but to seek out new growth opportunities"; and

4. Normative Goal Orientation, in which goals are set based on images of a desired future. Categorical planning, of course, is never as clean as the analyses done after the fact. Pittsfield's planning efforts, like all cities, contain aspects of each. In older industrial areas, however, it is the first category of Ameliorative Problem Solving that takes precedence because of the immediate financial needs of the community.

Anthropologists have a long history of involvement with societies undergoing rapid transformation. The impact of colonialism and European expansion set the stage for a discipline concerned with the stability and destruction of communities. Events in former colonial states, restrictions on research and funding, concern with what has been occurring in the United States and the realization that there are many similarities among those communities that have been studied abroad and those to be found in the United States, have moved many anthropologists to look at their own culture. This focus presents its own set of problems. I, for one, quickly discovered that I was not as familiar with my own culture as I assumed. Believing I knew the language, for example, it would be a while before I realized that I was ignorant of many meanings. Growing up in the Midwest, I discovered, was indeed different from experiencing the Northeast of the United States, which sometimes felt stranger, and more alienating, than foreign soil. Still, people did talk, and the results of this talk are presented here.

This book is organized to reflect the history and current conditions in the city of Pittsfield. Part 1 presents the theoretical umbrella of my argument about changes in the United States economy that have predicated Pittsfield's current position, and the relationship of that position to the global economy. Part 2 focuses on the current situation in Pittsfield and the attempts by residents to alleviate the crises that have occurred. Flowing through government structure to independent action, forms of resistance have arisen that are not normally noted in traditional analyses of communities in trouble.

In chapter 1, I situate Pittsfield. I present the rationale for choosing this community, arguing that many of the same processes that are occurring in Third World countries are present here as the dominant employer restructures and scales down production.

Chapters 2 and 3 present the community in the light of deindustrialization, downsizing, and relations of dependency. Using Gordon's (1996) excellent analysis of the bloated corporation, I hold here that the concept of deindustrialization is only partially sufficient for an understanding of the experience of communities losing their industrial base. What is more relevant is the way in which American corporations have reacted to entitlements won in past struggles by their workers. While workers have been downsized, as Gordon notes, managers have not, and the result has been the decreasing position of American productivity in relation to other individualized countries. Specifically, I propose that the formulation of "deindustrialization" does not adequately encompass megaindustrialziation on a local and global scale, and I present ideology as a primary component in the seduction of the community to maladaptive responses to the current crisis. Following Godfrey (1987) and Cardoso (1973), I further argue that the division between the First and Third World blurs as capital internalizes relations of dependent development irrespective of national boundaries.

In part 2, chapters 4 and 5 describe the arena in which the crises have occurred, both historically and at the present time. I have endeavored to present the points of view of the individuals and institutions involved, including the workers, voluntary associations, and the agents of the major corporation.

Chapter 6 outlines the history of development planning in Pittsfield. Development planning is a twentieth-century phenomenon, taking on particular significance in this area during the past twenty years.[3] The need for planning correlates directly with the community's experience with General Electric and decisions made by the corporation in its own global network. In Pittsfield, a commercial and marketing study was not done in the years between 1967 and 1987, symbolizing the stability of the Corporation during that period. When community leaders did begin the study in 1986, the city's government found itself trying to reconstruct the past as well as predict the future. The results of the city government's research and the results of "non-native" studies are analyzed in this chapter, pointing to the schisms between the corporate and community cycles of development.

I analyze the responses by different sectors of the population to differential power relations in the community. As parts of the community realign resources to adapt to these changing relationships, conflicts arise around the direction and implementation of development programs. The building of a mall and a "bypass" provide examples of projects that that development officials hoped would institute an "industrial revolution," while local businesses questioned the integrity of these initiatives. The processes by which conflicts are experienced result from a chaotic environment without leadership, and by mixed public relations messages produced by the corporation. Reactions to development proposals from development officers, local and regional politicians, corporate management and the area's workers and entrepreneurs point to the differential power resources attached to the ideologies presented. There is an assumption in the development literature that what is *good for economic indicators* is good for everyone, leading to a local assumption that what is good for GE is good for all (this belief brought about the local quip that when GE sneezes, Pittsfield gets the flu).

Chapter 7 describes a major response by the community to industrial restructuring by General Electric: the development of small kinship-based firms. Spawned from the entrepreneurial activities of one individual, these firms have seeded offshoots and products that have made them the major growth industry. The significance of this development is the kinship-based resistance to multinational restructuring.

The growth of these firms and the changes that are now affecting them have produced contradictions in belief and lifestyle for both the employers and employees. Even at their peak, employers cannot afford to provide the pay and benefits comparable to their own as union members working at the General Electric plant. There is competition for highly skilled employees and for sales accounts that provoke an atmosphere of secrecy and urgency. Movement to acquire these firms by outside conglomerates has produced its own set of schisms, just as competition on the international level has placed these firms in a precarious position.

Chapter 8 illustrates a case example of the deterioration of the social net and the consequences of power imbalances. Discussed here are the broader issues of health and the environment and their consequent influence on redevelopment efforts. Health has emerged as a major issue as the extent of toxic wastes in Pittsfield continues to be uncovered. Exploring how these issues are discussed and contested in the community, this case has implications for similar confrontations that are now taking place around the globe, the place of corporate responsibility and "corporate citizenship" in these discussions, and the role of ideology in the construction of "science."

The epilogue updates the responses of the community to actions by the major corporation since the 1980s. The trends noted in our fieldwork, conducted at the height of the restructuring of the corporation and of Pittsfield, have continued. Still, as with all ethnographic studies of communities, this book necessarily takes place in the "ethnographic present"—the time the research was done. But change is continual, and even if they appear the same, relationships change. I argue here that what happened in Pittsfield is not unique, updating the economic and social position of its residents while presenting implications for political action and policy analyses, along with a hope for the future.

Many will not agree with my interpretations or my conclusions. I am, like many of the "experts" hired to write reports and fix the ills of the area, an "outsider." Native views often differ from those of the researcher, and these differences need to be incorporated to provide an accurate picture of what has actually taken place.

And, as Eric Wolf tells us,

Anthropology in the past always operated among pacified or pacific natives: when the native "hits back" we are in a very different situation from that in which we found ourselves only yesterday. Thus the problem of power has suddenly come to the fore for us; and it exists in two ways—as power dominated exterted within our own system and as power exerted from the outside, often against us, by populations we so recently thought incapable of renewed assertion and resistance. (Wolf: 1974:258)

Written in 1974 about "traditional" anthropological fieldwork outside of the United States, the statement is even more to the point as anthropologists have begun to study their own cultures. Too many of us have reacted to the questioning of our analyses by an overconcern with cultural studies that abstractly interpret categories of difference. Yet at a time when academic disciplines are so concerned with dialogues and discourses of postmodernism and "meaning" pertaining to individuals and groups, on-the-ground ethnographic studies of rapid changes in the daily experience of people's lives are needed to show what happens to individuals and communities as economic restructuring, locally and globally, occurs.

It is my belief that "meaning" has gained too much attention in the social sciences without focus. Arthur Herman, in his *The Idea of Decline in Western History* (1997), even manages to argue that "decline" is relative, a word in the language of pessimists. Arguing that "meaning" is infinitely definable, what slips through the cracks in this postmodernist approach is the economy. This emphasis on meaning, I am convinced, is associated with the direction of power, manifested in Western culture by ignoring economic trends and reifying individual responsibility. It is a product of an ideology that reinforces the emphasis on the accumulation of capital at the true expense of families and communities.

I am concerned in this work with "experience," economic and otherwise, a level of analysis that points to changes in the way that people are able to lead their lives and fulfill their needs and dreams. I hope to show that changes in experience have proved traumatic for the citizens of Pittsfield, and that the catalysts for these changes are to be found in structural developments, not changes in attitudes or meaning as is often claimed by academics, corporate heads and development specialists. A discussion of attitudes and an interpretation of change alone would ignore concrete realities and deny the importance and the reality of the environment in which people operate, either adapting or resisting on a daily basis.

PART I

Problems and Issues

CHAPTER 1

The Chosen Community

The Community and its Setting

Until the 1980s, a tourist driving down the main street of Pittsfield could assume that the area was thriving. For those coming from New York or Boston, the downtown streets appeared exceptionally clean, homelessness was rare, and panhandlers almost nonexistent. Incorporated in 1891 with a total area of just over forty-two square miles and a population just under 49,000, the city had the appearance of many towns in upstate New York and southern New England: its low buildings of brick and wood built in the 1930s has the feel of Norman Rockwell's paintings of small-town America.

Economic restructuring has transformed the physical layout of Pittsfield and the lives of its inhabitants. This process is not bounded within the city limits. The main corporate employer is multinational; the tourists who come for skiing and summer leisure and the second home seekers that are buying available land arrive from regions and states far beyond the city's territory. Pittsfield is one of two cities in Berkshire County, with North Adams, about twenty-five miles to the north, its considerably smaller sister.

Today, the General Electric (GE) plant dominates the east side of town and has been the largest employer since the early part of the century. Its buildings span one whole side of the city, with the Shaeffer Eaton plant to the south dwarfed in comparison. Smaller manufacturing plants dot the landscape around and in Pittsfield, occupying old textile buildings as reminders of the city's history.

Electrical, electronics, and paper product manufacturers are the largest employers. Tourism runs a close second. Equidistant from New York and Boston, the area boasts over a hundred lakes and ponds and almost 85,000 acres of state reservation. The interchange between these mainstays of the

3

economy is a source of tension as the requirements of one often collided with those of the other.

The significant turnaround took place in the 1980s, when GE announced that it was scaling back its production of power transformers and was likely to cut production in other areas as well. The announcement coincided with the change in the appearance of North Street, once the city's main shopping district. A new mall, debated for forty years, finally encouraged store owners to abandon the storefronts they occupied. With the opening of the mall in the fall of 1988, North Street began to have the look of Cottrell's (1951) description of Caliente, the town that became obsolete with the development of the diesel locomotive engine. Englands department store, a symbol of retailing dedication to a community (the store granted long-term credit to GE workers during strikes), closed its doors in 1988, leaving the largest store on the street empty and disheveled. Though a hangout for teenagers, a Saturday morning finds the street and the entire downtown area with few pedestrians.

The physical changes that took place in the downtown area belie other transformations: an old movie house was in a state of disrepair; another became the Berkshire Public Theater. An abandoned store in an alleyway off the main street was turned into an art gallery, as was an old candy store. The second floor of one of the largest downtown buildings was made into studio space for the artists who exhibit in those galleries.

This is not the first time that structural change in the look and physical use of buildings has taken place in Pittsfield. The city transformed from a dying textile town into a thriving industrial center when the General Electric Corporation bought the Stanley Works in 1904, sustaining a dominant economic presence through most of the twentieth century. The shifts that have occurred since then—along with the international development of the corporation—have affected the town in dramatic ways. Old mill factories became the sites of small competitive factories, and later retail outlets. General Electric paid the highest wages for industrial work, attracting immigrants and later their families, and provided the health care and other benefits won in the union struggles and strikes during the past eight decades.

The thread that permeates through the changes in Pittsfield is dependency. The community is dependent on the corporation for the tax dollars that maintain the city infrastructure developed to house the plant and its workers; workers are dependent on the corporation for jobs; families on wage earners; and secondary industries on the wages that the workers generate. With General Electric as the largest employer in the area, Pittsfield can comfortably be called a "company town." Even the proliferation of the small industrial firms producing plastics products are linked by their history and workers to the General Electric plant. The current concern for redevelopment is intricately related to the role the corporation plays in the economy, and the role of the corporation in its own worldwide context.

Individuals and their families process the effects of these changes through an atmosphere of uncertainty. The expectation that children followed in the footsteps of their parents coincided with the certainty that General Electric paid the highest wages in the area. Children of long-term workers at the General Electric plant no longer depend on employment through family ties. Households swing between periodic employment at the plant and work at much lower-paid service jobs. There is no assurance of security, even for those workers with the most seniority. While managers make attempts to place laid-off workers in other positions at the plant, the closing down or restructuring of major areas of production leaves many skill-specific workers without recourse. The uncertainty about employment has created a strange reliance on "luck": workers see themselves as lucky to have jobs, families are lucky to have the money to pay their mortgages, individuals are lucky to be in good health.

Our interest in Pittsfield was in part due to the proliferation of small industries started by former General Electric employees. We assumed that how workers previously adapted to restructuring could inform present circumstances and point to ways that the community might view development efforts and its attempt to save the viability of the city.

Strong ethnic communities have solidified their kin-based ties through employment in the plant and entrepreneurial activities. Even when large divisions of the plant did restructure or close down, as was the case with the chemical division in the 1950s, strong community ties fostered by ethnic identity facilitated regrouping. From the start of one entrepreneurial small business grew a network of over thirty-eight small, competitive plastic injection and molding operations, enough to label Pittsfield the "Plastics Capital of America." General Electric is still the largest employer, with around 3,000 employees, followed by the Berkshire Medical Center with 1,800, the City of Pittsfield with 1,500, Kay Bee Toys with 350, and the Berkshire Life Insurance Company with 350.

The substantial changes occurring in the 1980s resulted in a gradual erosion of the community base. The population has steadily declined during the past two decades as children move to other areas and workers migrate in the hope of finding work in sunnier climes; rumors of a major part of the plant's closing down have been realized; the hope of the community—the plastic's industry—has been threatened by foreign competition and cyclical downturns. The city government is divided over development issues, and development managers do not have long tenures. Issues concerning the use and abuse of the environment, as well as the effect of chemicals used in the production process, have come to a head as segments of the community are pitted against each other on fundamental issues of human health.

The city's struggle to restructure its economic base embodies community conflict. General Electric maintains that it is still committed to the area, citing the placement of its international plastics headquarters there in the mid-1980s. The center, based on research and development, employs only a small number of workers and is overshadowed by the public relations text generated for the community. The tensions created in the community become more apparent as economic stability erodes. The Chamber of Commerce promotes the area as one of scenic rural beauty and rare cultural opportunities. The literature designed to attract industry describes the lush hills and crisp air that has long attracted summer residents to Lenox and Stockbridge in the south and Williamstown and to the hill towns of the north. Tanglewood, Shakespaere and Company, Jacob's Pillow, and the Williamstown and Berkshire Theater festivals draw substantial numbers from New York City and Boston, just as the fall foliage and winter skiing jam the roadways into the growing number of resort towns.

City government and development agencies realize that tourism alone will not solve the city's budget problems. But there is a desperation inherent in current planning: a need to quickly generate money to offset the sudden tax decreases caused by General Electric's scaling down of production. The tourist and second home industries resist new initiatives that will potentially pollute the environment, just as any open confrontation that might further compromise the community's relationship with the corporation is avoided. Thus, the major fights that have evolved are not over how to attract industry but rather about the placement of income-generating parking garages and the building of shopping malls within or outside the city limits.

Community leaders and consultants locate the creation of economic stability in the realm of new development. What this means in the context of underlying economic change and adaptive response is the subject of this work.

CHAPTER 2

Community and Context

> There was this Englishman who worked in the London
> office of a multinational corporation based in the United
> States. He drove home one evening in his Japanese car.
> His wife, who worked in a firm which imported German
> kitchen equipment, was already at home. Her small Italian
> car was often quicker through the traffic. After a meal
> which included New Zealand lamb, California carrots,
> Mexican honey, French cheese and Spanish wine, they set-
> tled down to watch a programme on their television set,
> which had been made in Finland. The programme was a
> retrospective celebration of the war to recapture the
> Falkland Islands. As they watched it they felt warmly patri-
> otic, and very proud to be British.
>
> Raymond Williams, *The Year 2000*

The experience of dependency on a major employer is a delicate balance predicated on an understanding of both the community and the company's needs. As in Pittsfield, the American experience has been one of towns and cities building their infrastructures around the physical prerequisites of industry that, in turn, hires its citizens and provides the tax base to keep the community afloat. With the restructuring of capitalism around the globe, this relationship has changed. Cities and towns find themselves providing incentives and tax breaks they can ill afford to keep industry within their borders; companies threaten to leave areas at the slightest hint of labor unrest. The balance that used to exist between corporate and community management is no longer respected by heads of corporations, who are, more often than not, far from the plant site.

This imbalance generates a series of confusing alternatives for communities trying to keep their infrastructures afloat. Corporate managers, who

are, however temporarily, citizens of these communities, may try to negotiate with corporate headquarters to keep production intact, but more often
than not they fail to convince their superiors unless they can provide financial incentives that compete with planned operations. The pretense of the
corporation is that they are doing their best and are committed to the community. The reality is the deindustrialization and downsizing that has characterized the current economic decline.

The emphasis on new development by city planners assumes that
restructuring has taken place or is well under way. The flight of industry
from northern to southern cities and to other parts of the globe has devas-
tated the infrastructure of entire regions and has left unemployed entire segments of the population dependent on industrial work. The hardest hit are
the old, northern, industrial cities that flourished during the industrial revolution and survived the restructuring of industry after the Second World War.

The Growth of the American City

The rise of the modern American city is closely bound to the fluctuations of
capitalist development during the last half of the nineteenth century and the
twentieth century. Gordon (1984) posits that American cities have passed
through three stages of development—the commercial, the industrial, and
the corporate—and that each of these stages corresponds to dynamics of
capitalist accumulation during that period (1984:22).[1] The commercial city,
based on merchant accumulation, used the city as trading centers for the
exchange of commodities. Political capitals or colonial control centers
served to regulate market privileges and housed the entrepreneurs and
craftspeople who migrated there to produce the luxury goods consumed by
capitalist traders. Ports served as transportation centers. The early development of these cities were regulated by the British Crown, which kept control
over the size and distribution of port cities. With the coming of independence, American merchants took control of the commercial functions of the
cities and the number and size of port cities expanded rapidly, along with a
distinct urban population.[2]

Gordon places the transition between the commercial and the industrial
city and its corresponding forms of accumulation between 1850 and 1870.
Cities grew as propertyless laborers and unemployed craftsmen flocked to
central areas. The first industrial cities were centered on the riverbanks of
New England, tied to the use of water as the main power source.[3] With the
transition to coal and the development of railroads as a major source of transportation between 1850 and 1870, industry became located in large cities
with ample labor to meet the growing demand for factory production. Large
cities functioned to better control the labor force, a factor that had become

increasingly difficult in small and medium-sized cities that contained militant pockets of resistance to industrial discipline.[4] The greater physical separation of workers and owners and the increased impersonality of the city worked in favor of the capitalist industrial enterprise. With factories located in the center of the urban areas, the upper classes, with more access to transportation and leisure time, moved out of the cities into newly developing suburbs. At the same time, however, this concentration of industry in the urban areas was creating contradictions for capitalist accumulation. The rapid rise of factories created a demand for labor, which increased wages, and for worker organization. During the last decades of the nineteenth century, resistance to capitalist discipline grew and substantially threatened capitalist control over production.

The corporate city developed in response to growing instability as manufacturing migrated from central cities to the outer rings around the urban areas. As Gordon tells us, "Between 1899 and 1909, central-city manufacturing employment increased by 40.8 percent while ring employment rose by 97.7 percent" (1984:40). With the movement of manufacturing out of the city, central city areas were reorganized as business districts coordinating the administrative aspects of capitalist trade. Corporations, after the First World War I, had grown enough to separate administration from the sites of production and skyscrapers housing corporate headquarters flourished in the major cities around the country. The dispersal of industrial production also scattered and diffused working-class neighborhoods, militating against the community-based pockets of resistance that had been organizing during the late nineteenth century.

The form of the corporate city took shape in the first half of the twentieth century and became solidified with the hegemony of the United States after the Second World War. Defense spending and the growth of transportation increased the strength of corporate holdings and allowed the expansion to new cities while decapitalizing the old. The move to new cities was both the result of aging physical plants and increasing union organization. New cities were loci of nonunion labor and wide open spaces. With hegemonic control over vast areas of the world system, United States–based corporations also started to expand their operations overseas. Increasing improvements in technology have allowed for the organization of production around the globe with unskilled or semiskilled labor and have opened up new arenas for capitalist control. Along with these developments, however, are major changes in the economic structure of U.S. cities and regular cycles of crisis, particularly in the older cities, but expanding to the new ones as well. These changes have prompted growing social problems and challenges to large segments of the populations dependent on factory production and its offshoots.

CHAPTER 3

Restructuring, Megaindustrialization, and the Expansion of the Service Sector

"Deindustrialization," "downsizing," and "restructuring" are the buzzwords of the 1980s and 1990s. The language refers to attempts by corporations to increase their profit margin, often relocating or severely cutting their employee base to do so. It is important to note that while ideologically justified by the corporate responsibility to "stockholders," these organizational shifts more often succeed in lining the pockets of lawyers and Wall Street executives while diminishing the living standards of the majority of Americans.

David Gordon (1996) argues in his *Fat and Mean* that there is another reason for the flurry of activity that is reorganizing corporate structures: their strategy to limit the power of employees to seek shares in the rewards of work and to increase the power and earnings of corporate management. Downsizing is specific to hourly employees. Managerial bloat has grown throughout the 1980s and 1990s, while squeezing the wages of workers. While after-tax spendable hourly earnings have decreased for production and nonsupervisory employees by 8.6 percent between 1979 and 1994, real hourly earnings have decreased by 9.8 percent (Gordon, 1996:31). On the other hand, the percentage of administrative and managerial employees increased from 6.6 percent to 13 percent between 1960 and 1989 in the United States, contrasting with Sweden's 2.6 percent, Japan's 4.2 percent, and Germany's 3.9 percent in 1989 (1996:47). The United States lags behind Belgium, Canada, Denmark, France, Germany, Italy, Japan, Netherlands, Norway, Sweden, and the United Kingdom in the change in real hourly compensation for manufacturing employees between 1973 and 1993.[1] Ideology machines respond by changing the statistics. A commission appointed by the

11

Senate Finance Committee in 1996 claims, for example, that income is actually rising. It performed this feat by simply changing the Consumer Price Index to reflect what it calls "overstated inflation," thus concluding that there has been a .02 percent increase per year in household earnings between 1973 and 1995. Despite the rejection of this analysis by the majority of economists who support the data showing a steady decline, the government insists that it depicts a rise in the standard of living. "How can the (former) data be accurate," the *New York Times* quotes Jerry Jasonowski, president of the National Association of Manufacturers as saying, "when corporate America is performing so well?" (*New York Times*, February 23, 1997). The irony is obviously lost on those who would like to insist that Americans are doing well, despite the qualifier by the former chief of the Bureau of Labor Statistics Consumer Price Index division, who told the reporter that "this new living standard is beyond the reach of an increasing proportion of Americans" (*New York Times*, February 23, 1997).

These trends have consequences for U.S. employees, and they also have repercussions for the economy as a whole. While living standards plummet, so do trade deficits and productivity ratios. Unhappy employees do not make good workers. Americans have lost confidence in U.S. corporations, with only a striking 16 percent expressing confidence in U.S. companies in 1993.[2]

The attack on wage compensation for nonsupervisory employees is not new and has taken different forms during the twentieth century. During the period of fieldwork in Pittsfield, managerial strategies took the form of movement—away from areas where workers expected to be paid reasonable rates to areas where corporations believed they could get "a better deal." The result was deindustrialization, the lowering of wage scales for the majority of U.S. workers, and in many cases, the destruction of communities.

The basis for deindustrialization, Barry Bluestone and Bennett Harrison tell us, is the way "capital—in the forms of financial resources and of real plant and equipment—has been diverted from productive investment in our basic national industries into unproductive speculation, mergers and acquisitions, and foreign investment" (1982:6). The switch from corporate investment in basic production to investment in financial speculation has forecast the shutdown of factories in U.S. regions dependent on factory stability and growth. As authors of this study note, the process of deindustrialization in the United States during the 1970s cost American workers some 38 million jobs, and the chance of a large, established plant closing down during that period in the United Stated reached 30 percent (Bluestone and Harrison, 1982:9).

Deindustrialization results when capital investment shifts away from the industrial sector to other sectors of the economy or overseas. By closing down plants and disinvesting in constant capital, large multinational corporations have decapitalized basic industry during the last twenty years in the United States. These companies have not, however, discontinued investment in production. General Electric, Pittsfield's largest employer, expanded during the 1970s, adding 30,000 foreign jobs while decreasing domestic employment by 25,000. The Ford Motor Company followed suit, spending more than 40 percent of its capital budget outside the United States (Bluestone and Harrison, 1982:9).

Like downsizing and managerial bloat, deindustrialization is a result of corporate managerial strategies to threaten American workers and keep them under control (what Gordon refers to as "the stick strategy"). Demands for an increased share of the profits by American workers are met with the movement of capital to areas with less overt resistance and lower labor costs. International competition leads to the abandonment of production by American companies in favor of more lucrative investments in finance capital and the service sector.

The loss of industry and the growth of the service sector has led researchers to view American society as "post industrial." This view, however, neglects to account for new forms of industrialization. The economic analysis of deindustrialization is better understood as industrial restructuring linked to cycles of capitalist development. The restructuring of industry is not a new phenomenon on the American economic scene, and the deindustrialization of basic industry in local areas is just one side of the phenomenon. What is occurring in Late Capitalism is a process of *megaindustrialization*—where "mechanization, standardization, over-specialization and parcellization of labor, which in the past determined only the realm of commodity production in actual industry, now penetrate into all sectors of social life" (Mandel, 1972:387). Televisions replace teachers in schools; newspapers are replaced by soundbites. With the industrialization of service, the deskilling of work Braverman (1972) described as characteristic of capitalist enterprises extends to new areas. The electrocardiogram allows the employment of a lower-paid technician rather than a doctor; automated credit machines replace manual checks; Polaroid cameras do away with the need for the manual processing of film. Even finance companies have improved ways to manipulate capital: the development of mutual funds makes obsolete the need for one-at-a-time stock transactions. In short, the private relationship between the seller of labor power that constitutes a service and the buyer of that service becomes a specifically capitalist phenomenon.[3] The myth that technology has eased the burden of employees is contradicted by the real fall in wages and the increased profit of a tiny minority of the population.

While the industrial sector has restructured, the service sector has grown by leaps. Characterized by low wages and minimal skill levels, this change is rationalized by economists as making industrialization efficient on a world scale. Moves to areas of low-wage expectation increases productivity. As assembly lines replace crafts and supermarkets replace retail stores, less labor and less skilled labor are required. While relative productivity increases, jobs are lost and living standards fall. Productivity, in other words, means profit, and profit is not evenly distributed. The growth of the service sector follows from the growing specialization of the world division of labor. Mandel notes that

> a growing division of labor can only be combined with growing objective socialization of the labor process by an extension of *intermediate functions*, hence the unprecedented expansion of the sectors of commerce, transport and services generally. *Economically*, the process of centralization can only find expression in a growing centralization of capital, among other things, in the form of vertical integration of big companies, multinational firms and conglomerates." (1972:383)

He argues that the growth of the service sector is, in part, due to the growing problems presented by the "realization" of capital—the continuing expansion of capital and its realization into profits and surplus value. The creation and production of new commodities require that needs be created to motivate consumption. Thus, while intermediate functions are required to administrate new forms of capital intervention worldwide, the functions of sales and advertising are also needed to persuade people to buy products. There has been an enormous expansion both of selling costs and consumer credit. While strategically successful, these movements have created their own problems. There is now more credit available for the American population than ever before. There are also more bankruptcies. The advertizing and credit that promise a better life do not correspond with the fall in wages and lack of resources available for consumption. While the government administration praises the growth of the economy and the stock market hits new heights, there is an economic crisis marching on for the average American.

Megaindustrialization and Merger Movements

As the further "rationalization" of capital and service industries takes place, small industries are incorporated and replaced by large conglomerates that more "efficiently" manage capital from the various sectors of the economy. The enormous increase in corporate mergers reflects attempts to "rationalize" the manipulation and investment of capital. The up and down swings of capitalist expansion are caused, as Bergensen notes, by excessive competition and overproduction: "The resolution to this blockage in the accumulation process is crisis and downturn, where the failure of individual firms and the elimination of others through mergers allows the accumulation process to move forward again" (Bergersen, 1982:28).[4]

Bergensen places the period 1945–73 as the locus of another long swing of expansion that witnessed the growth of multinationals and overseas development and the recession of 1974–75 and 1980 as a period of sluggish growth. He predicted at the date of his writing that a general crisis of accumulation would result in a new round of mergers, a prediction borne out in the last half of the 1980s. However, the overspecialization of corporate strategies has prevented multinationals from competing with a new form of merger—the state-owned enterprise. Begensen provides as an example the 1982 state-ordered consolidation of three auto plants in South Korea, positing that "If we argue that the leading capitalist state will not be able to adjust successfully to the present downturn, nowhere is this failure better seen than in trying to imagine how the American Government could 'order' the merger of, for example, Ford, GE and Chrysler" (Bergensen, 1982:35). What has happened instead is the mega-mergers of multinational companies, with U.S. auto companies buying out foreign competition, health maintenance organizations merging with hospitals, and insurance and electronic corporations, in general, combining in the hope of "rationalizing" their production. The state-owned enterprises are now competing with multinationals.[5] In the meantime, these mega-mergers are creating a boom on Wall Street, where single individuals are pulling in fees and commissions in the hundreds of millions of dollars.

As the industrialization of service and the intensive capitalization of all sectors of society takes place, Mandel observes, it expands areas of investment while containing arenas of class struggle. As multinationals confront increased competition from state-owned firms around the world, increasing attempts are made to lower the labor cost through the movement of firms or the lowering of wages and the retraction of entitlements. While administrative structures or divisions concerned with research and development may remain in the United States because of the need for specialized knowledge and facilities, those multinationals unsuccessful in renegotiating employee demands will attempt to move production elsewhere.[6] The result is the creation of a new labor force that is more highly bifurcated on both ends of the spectrum.

This change in the structure of the labor force has changed the habits of consumption. While middle-class families are replaced by two-income households, both working at minimum wage, there is a vastly growing market for luxury goods, fueled by grossly inflated incomes on the other end of the scale.

The rapid proliferation of malls with upper-income stores and gourmet restaurants during the last half of the 1980s is a clear indication that a substantial luxury market does exist. In Pittsfield, this picture is mitigated by the specific nature of the community's history as well as its geographic placement between a major world city (New York) and a large northeastern financial and educational center (Boston). The mall built in the Pittsfield area could not attract the upscale stores that it desired—much of the shopping for luxury goods is outside the area.[7]

The bifurcation of the labor force in Pittsfield, however, is evident. The placement of General Electric's International Plastics headquarters in Pittsfield has accentuated the change in production from basic industry to research and design on the one hand (a process June Nash [1989] has labeled *From Tank Town to High Tech*) to the proliferation of service sector jobs on the other. The mall, with some of the only employment opportunities in the area, still had trouble finding enough individuals to work for the wages it offered as sales and maintenance personnel.

The transfer of capital by corporations searching for lower labor and production costs produces competition among communities attracting industry. Communities threatened with the loss of jobs attempt to win corporate moves to their area or keep local industry intact by offering tax "vacations"—abatements that limit the corporation's responsibility to the community as well as their financial contribution. While this tactic does sometimes succeed in persuading companies not to relocate, the tax burden necessary to maintain the infrastructure of the community becomes the additional problem of already overburdened government budgets. The threatened or real movement of capital overseas has generated a new wave of hostilities by American workers against foreign governments and peoples who are perceived to be taking the remaining life-sustaining jobs that are fast disappearing from the American scene.

The loss of jobs caused by downsizing and the movement of capital out of the United States is multiplied by other industries that are affected by industry shutdown and by the tax losses of the community. As Bluestone and Harrison projected, "the 8,000 jobs potentially lost nationwide in the automobile industry ultimately cause a decline in employment among all industries of more than 20,600. In other words, more than 12,000 non-auto industry jobs would be affected. . . . The Massachusetts Office of Economic Affairs has developed a rule of thumb according to which every $10,000 salary level job lost to the state costs it about $1,336 in foregone state and local taxes" (Bluestone and Harrison, 1982:71–73).

This reorientation in capital investment has produced a shift in employment rates within the global economy. Unemployment in the most industrialized countries has overtaken those of developing nations (Godfrey, 1986).

Neo-Keynesian predictions for full employment (defined as unemployment rates between 4 and 7 percent) appeared to be reaching reality during the 1960s in the most advanced countries, only to quickly fall as offshore sourcing became the favored method of reducing labor costs. It is reaching reality again in the 1990s with a serious caveat. The jobs becoming available are low-paying, do not offer health benefits, and do not provide security. The Keynsian model does not account for the *type* of employment necessary for a healthy economy, and present statistics do not reflect the real fall in the standard of living, or the crises in health and social services that have followed.

It became clear early on in our case study that the issues of "redevelopment" and economic restructuring are integrated through the processes of capitalist accumulation on a world scale. For the residents of Pittsfield, disivestment in basic industry by General Electric had drastic effects on the community. General Electric workers specifically trained for industrial work found themselves transferred to jobs outside their speciality or laid off with little chance of finding work paying the same wage; city leaders faced with reduced tax revenues scrambled with contradictory development orientations and a fragmented city government; the downtown area of the city deteriorated. Deindustrialization in Pittsfield is further complicated by quickly rising land values—the result of the "overconsumption" characteristic of the class of managers, professionals, and credentialed technicians that is being hired by General Electric and others who are coming into the area from New York and Boston to buy second homes. Many long-time residents find that while the value of their homes has increased exponentially, their real incomes have fallen.

Specific results of the restructuring processes—whether it be the increased alienation or disemployment of labor in the General Electric plant or the production of chaos in the planning arms of city government—are linked to the activities of the corporate mechanism of the corporation at its headquarters in Fairfield, Connecticut, its world plastics headquarters in Pittsfield, or one of the many subsidiaries around the globe. In a world where sovereign nations represent, for multinational corporations, not much more than a map line for demarcating boundaries, the analysis of crisis has become surprisingly localized in the social sciences. To analyze the local scene without the acknowledgment of these pressures results in a myopic view of social process.

The members of the community interviewed for this study—the workers at the plant, the owners of the plastics firms, the members of city government, and the heads of social service agencies—were well aware of the global scope of the corporation if not the direct effects of global strategies on the community. Workers involved with the union tend to be more aware of the global workplace then do those who have lost faith in union activity or found themselves employed in service sector jobs. The owners of the small plastics firms were the most aware of the global nature of production—a result of the direct competition they were experiencing from offshore sourcing.

These interviews convinced us that the theoretical constructs of deindustrialization and downsizing do not provide adequate tools to describe what was happening in Pittsfield or other communities in the United States. The use of a broader category, such as "restructuring," is more descriptive of the processes of change involved in capitalist accumulation, but does not provide a framework to describe what is being restructured and why. The analyses that use these units of analysis most often focus on the corporation at the expense of the community, describing one side of a complex process that is reshaping the everyday lives of community residents. It is here that anthropology can make a contribution, by analyzing the relationships among people that include the elements of power that structure the lives of individuals. Rather than viewing the "individual units" of deindustrialized communities, the scope of anthropology should entail relating the diverse forces of society that intersect the whole.

Constructing Consensus in Late Capitalism

Wolf (1974) argues that anthropology, following dominant intellectual themes, has not incorporated aspects of power into analyses of social systems and organizations. Under that capitalist mode of production the idea of 'power' has become so intertwined with notions of 'property' that the relationships of dominance inherent in ownership have become subsumed under the rubric of 'the right to own.' An ideology of the freedom of labor that capitalism accomplished allowed a control over production by individuals with capital to buy labor power. It also allowed individuals to sell their labor with the freedom of geographic movement that labor as a commodity provides. Thus workers were free to sell their labor while capitalists were free to buy it—presenting a façade of equalitarian relationships. In the United States, this ideology of equalitarianism is backed by the fight for independence from a colonial power and the right of all to own property formerly held by the colonial forces. All were thus free to become rich—as Warner shows in his analysis of Memorial Day (1953), the central symbols in this "American sacred ceremony" are those of equalitarianism and the rags-to-riches myth that has become a staple of American culture.

Williams demonstrates in *The Year 2000* (1983b) that the evolution of capitalism brought with it an idea of labor in market terms. The industrial revolution began an association of work with employment and has solidified since the Second World War. As he notes, unemployment has become endemic to the older industrial states, and so has mass employment—the majority of individuals in the United States are involved in the labor force and that participation is still at historically high levels. Those who employ labor are said to be "self-employed"— a sentiment that again places the owner of labor on the same equalitarian plane as the worker.

The ideology of work as employment is a tenet of American life. Failure to gain employment and a decent wage is necessarily the problem of the worker, not the system or owner who employs the labor. In his handbook for American workers assigned overseas, Arensberg (n.d.) counseled that foreign conceptions of work may not be the same as our own that are tied into ideas of success and achievement.[8]

This dominant ideology is a by-product of modernization theory, used to justify the intervention of capital overseas during the 1950s and 1960s, although it is now readily practiced by U.S. corporations as well. Modernization theory posits that restructuring leading to corporate growth is a naturally recurring phenomenon, and impediments to it are "attitudinal" in scope. Populations need to be convinced of the necessity and the naturalness of economic change. If they cannot adapt, they will suffer. For company towns such as Pittsfield that function virtually as single-commodity cities, the failures of the relations of production to satisfy human needs are attributed to perception, individual failure, or community "backwardness." Here the construction of consensus is approached through the discourse of successes and failures of the community to respond to market trends and the needs of the capitalist enterprise.

The way this ideology is played out is dependent on existing social relations of production. In Third World regions with a history of exploitation and colonial rule, the military plays a prominent role in enforcing ideological standards. In "more developed" countries such as the United States with a history of worker organization, ideology has a more social face, with attempts at consensus constructed through ideas of right and wrong and the creation of needs as a consumer.

The schism between the moral tone attributed to employment and the realities of the laws of capital are striking. The drive for profit by which capitalism depends necessarily ignores human needs beyond consumption. Health, education, crime, job satisfaction, and community life are all categories that do not neatly fit into analyses of productivity. The United States is currently experiencing economic growth unparalleled in the past thirty years. Yet the social crises that are present are mounting and unaccounted for. The answer, according to the U.S. government, is to destroy the social net entirely. Economic growth is healthy, President Clinton claims, while welfare is not. Education is challenged with the most damaging crises it has ever encountered, with only lip service being paid to the phenomenon. While numerous studies link the need for education and social security to long-term economic health, short-term planning and profit motivation overshadow hard realities.

PART II

A New England Community in Crisis

CHAPTER 4

The Region and Industry in History

The unifying theme among Pittsfield's residents is economic security. Laid-off workers or those who face termination from the General Electric plant hope for increased sales of their product or defense contracts from the federal government; government leaders hope to attract new industry; and store owners hope that the influx of tourists and second home owners will stimulate merchandise sales. Most importantly, economic security means the successful maintenance of family and property.

In Pittsfield, as in much of the United States, the protection of a secure economic base for the security of family and community is at odds with the cycles of industrialization. From the early years of factory life, the family was increasingly de-emphasized as a driving force in the economic life of communities even as struggles to maintain its integrity has figured high in resistance to the capitalist mode of production. Union organizations became important for the protection of material security and for emotional support as families lost their power to make decisions affecting their members.

Early Industrialization and New England Social Structure

The history of New England demonstrates that economic productivity is not necessarily the result of natural resources. Eisenmenger (1967) notes that New England has limited resources (primarily of pulpwood, limestone, and granite), its land is not inherently productive, and wide temperature variations result in fuel costs substantially higher than in the rest of the country. While the region's ports were a major factor in shaping the economy in the eighteenth and nineteenth centuries, the ports of New York, Philadelphia, and Baltimore took over the majority of shipping business on the eastern seaboard during the twentieth century (Eisenmenger 1967:3).

Textile manufacturing transformed New England in the nineteenth century, with seaports providing access to raw materials and overseas markets. The War of 1812 relaxed the mercantilist restrictions of European powers, giving the United States access to international markets and stimulating economic growth. Cotton played a decisive role in the development of the Atlantic trade, which financed much of America's industrialization. With the West of the United States still largely unintegrated into the national economy, the booms and busts of the cotton trade were the main influence in American economic growth (North, 1966).

United States interregional trade grew substantially with the introduction of the Mississipi steamboat in 1816, opening up affordable trade between the South and the West (North, 1966:102). The initial result of this expansion of trade was a solidification of the division of labor among the regions of the West, the South, and the Northeast. A process of uneven and combined development took hold as U.S. industry adopted technology and relations of production from England, recruiting labor and organizing factory work in accordance with the needs of particular commodities (Burawoy, 1985:100). The expanding national market and an intensification of agriculture depopulated the countryside and brought farmers into urbanizing settlements where even the famous New England town meeting would disappear (Fink, 1987:251). From 1820 to 1860, the American workforce was quickly transformed from agricultural pursuits to industrial concerns. An increase from 28 to 41 percent of the United States population became employed outside of agriculture during this period (Dublin, 1979). New England, with internal migration and external immigration filling the towns and cities, would gain the distinction of having the longest history of wage labor in the United States.

New England had a dramatic shift to employment in textile production during the mid-1800s. The workers, once agricultural, encountered a class of textile manufacturing owners who were both closely allied with one another and aware of the lifestyles and needs of their workers.[1] Paternalistic practices served to provide rhetoric and incentive for the disciplining and the socialization of the workforce, as owners provided cash gifts, responded to family crises, and allayed the natural suspicions toward manufacturing owners, insuring the reproduction of the workforce through family ties. Families served as a haven and "a continuing refuge against the pressures of factory discipline" (Prude, 1987:95). The efforts by mill owners to socialize their workers did not prevent the new emerging working class from using their own traditions to adapt the workplace and their new communities. Hareven (1975) shows how family traditions and corporations interacted to produce viable economic projects, while rejecting the "revisionist sociological view" of the family as an independent unit in the process of industrialization.[2] The work of Herbert Gutman and his peers show how "traditional" styles of behavior were integrated or acted as cataclysts of resistance to industrialization in the United States in the same way that anthropologists have demonstrated this phenomenon for other areas of the world (cf. Nash, 1979).[3]

The Amoskeag Mill in southern New Hampshire is representative of the factories of the time, and we have a record of its operations through the work of Hareven and Langenbach (1975). Here, the largest ethnic groups in the workforce were French Canadians, who had the highest birth rate of all industrial workers in the United States (1975:45), and Scotch workers recruited directly from their home communities. For the workers in the late 1800s, the plant became a living entity that hired, fired, fed, and clothed its members.

The success of the textile mills may have as much to do with cultural traditions as with manipulated work ethics. The large families of the French Canadians worked well in factory as in farmwork, and the work ethics of the migrants blended easily from family time into industrial time. As one of Hareven and Langenbach's informants who came to Amoskeag employed as a weaver commented:

> When I came in 1900, we worked from six in the morning till six at night. I worked solid. My Aunt, she wouldn't allow any gallivanting around. Even on the weekends I worked. But I liked it from the start. The ups were all right, and the downs were all right. I liked weaving. (Hareven and Langenbach, 1978:44)

References to Amoskeag were made as to an animate object.[4] The paternalistic operations of the company allowed for a personality. Hareven and Langenbach's same informant tells them:

> One day the Amoskeag fired me. I didn't watch the loom, and it was running away from me. They fired me for that. I got another job weaving the same day. I was young at the time, about eighteen. Aunt Susan used to get after me. She'd say, "You don't keep your mind on your work. Your mind's somewhere else, and of course you get confused." If you were fired, you'd have to go to some other mill—Amoskeag had twelve mills you know,—but you'd find another job. You see, your old boss wouldn't hire you back right away. If he had a recollection of firing you, he wouldn't do it for quite a while. (1978:47)

In the work world of Amoskeag, the tasks performed were diversified, giving the workers a knowledge of the overall process. Entire families worked in the same factory; the family unit acted as housing coordinators and labor recruiters. The workplace fostered comradery among employees that heightened their sense of community responsibility and stretched beyond domestic ties. The demand and competition for labor meant that the corporation was more open to worker's demands, and Amoskeag in 1910, well before other American corporations, instituted benefit plans that allowed workers to own homes, keep their teeth in order, and care for their children. At the same time, however, scientific management was streamlining the production process, a process of class struggle that would spark mass resistance in the twentieth century.

The period between 1830 and 1850 was one of sustained growth in the textile industry with the introduction of the power loom from England. The wool industry became highly localized in New England, and Massachusetts assumed the premiere role for cotton mills (North, 1966:163). The characteristics of the milling technology and a growing market for coarse fabrics induced industries to organize by an economy of scale, the technology suitable for recruitment of female laborers who could be housed together, paid less then men and reliably socialized as a workforce (Burawoy, 1985:101).[5] Dublin tells us that women had a "respected place in the pre-industrial economy of the north, but [it] placed severe limits on their independence" (1979:3). Work for females was much like migration for men, allowing for self-sufficiency and access to commodities unavailable in their nonindustrial lives. Daughters living at home kept a portion of their incomes, encouraging economic and social independence (1979:42).

Production in New England, then, was reinforced by a tradition of family and community that was well adapted for industry. Historians have surmised that the social structure and sanctions of the period made the United States particularly hospitable for the pursuit of economic gain through manufacturing (North, 1966:vi). The commitment of the labor force and the willingness to work allowed New England to dominate the commercial economy of the country in the early decades of the nineteenth century. By 1840 Massachusets stood third in per capita income at $107, with the national average at $65, and the other southern New England states of Rhode Island and Connecticut ranking first and fourth, respectively. A third of United States manufacturing employment was in this region (Eisenmenger, 1967:18).

A lack of capital for good rail connections, the discovery of gold, and the expansion of the West proved a disadvantage to New England manufacturers after 1850. A revolution in the design and manufacture of textile machinery freed manufacturers from their reliance on New England labor (Harrison, 1982:16). Parts became standardized and interchangeable. In much the same fashion that Hobsbawm's (1964) managers reacted to gas workers in late-nineteenth-century England by transforming the organic composition of capital, New England manufacturers confronting unionized shops and seeking cheaper labor, deskilled production tasks and moved to the southeastern states. Owners no longer needed paternalistic practices to keep their workers productive—the proverbial stick and carrot was replaced by the threat to close down and relocate.

Relations of Work and Unemployment

Despite the atmosphere of relative calm characterizing the early mills, unemployment was a continual problem. Steady work was a rarity for mill workers, who experienced over a 30 percent unemployment rate as early as 1885 in Massachusetts (Keyssar, 1987:233). Craftsmen and women banded together to protect their interests in their work and to protect their families against the vagaries of industrial employment. Labor organizations struggled to form coherent organizations to confront increased demands by owners, but most resistance took place among individual craftsmen in the workplace (Montgomery 1979:13).

Organized labor did succeed in becoming institutionalized between the Civil War and the First World War, giving Massachusetts the longest history of labor unions in the United States (Montgomery, 1979:234). The radicalism of the working class, however, was dampened by the shortage of available jobs, and Keyssar estimates that between 1881 and 1900 "roughly one out of every six strikers in the Commonwealth lost his or her job to a new employee" (1979: 236).[6] The availability of new immigrants as a constant source of cheap labor together with the expansion of the West, along with the importation and development of new technologies, militated against resistance and conditioned the character of the U.S. labor movement in a way that European workers would not experience until the late twentieth century. It has in turn provided fuel for debates about "why the U.S. working class is different." Workers were well aware of the sources of their fluctuating security and some advocated the abolition of capitalism.[7] In some areas—such as Fall River, Massachusetts—unions were successful enough to determine wages and close down plants, leading one treasurer of a Fall River mill to comment during a strike in 1870 that "the question with the spinners was not wages, but whether they or the manufacturers should rule. For the last six or eight years they have ruled Fall River" (quoted in Montgomery, 1979:18). Unions acted to redistribute wages through union benefits and often to regulate the pace of work in an effort to preserve jobs. The plumbers union, for example, ruled that bicycles were forbidden as a means of transportation between jobs in their belief that there was not enough work to go around, while the moldmakers union "legislated" that their members were not to report to work before seven in the morning (Montgomery, 1979:16).

The decline of textiles in the late nineteenth and early twentieth century generated unrest even in the communities that formerly had unconditionally supported the textile firms. The family units that worked so well together in the factories also found themselves together out of work. At Amoskeag resistance that prompted a nonviolent strike in 1922 escalated and turned violent in 1933, bringing in the state militia. By 1933, as the third generation of immigrant families had workers in the factories, the deterioration of labor relations had proved unworkable for smooth factory operations at Amoskeag, with workers complaining of being "worked to death."

The fate of Amoskeag is similar to many of the textile mills in New England. The number of manufacturing jobs in Massachusetts dropped significantly between 1920 and 1929, hitting hardest the shoe and textile industries. The increased competition from plants in the South forced the closing of plants in all parts of Massachussets, leaving tens of thousands of workers unemployed.[8] Workers sought work by running ahead of the plant closings in the hope of gaining employment. As Hareven and Langdenbach report, "Each time a new textile plant opened, former Amoskeag workers would rush to the gates, hoping that some of their former bosses would recognize them and hire them. Many got into a mill only to find themselves outside again. Lucille Bourque summarized the long history of uncertainty: 'After the Amoskeag I went to the Raylaine and the Raylaine closed. I went to Textron, and that closed. And then I quit. I used to go in and out. I'd quit and go back' " (Hareven and Langenbach, 1978:306).

By the mid-1930s, a full one-quarter of the labor force in Massachusetts was unemployed, while an additional 10 percent was working part-time (Keyssar, 1986:289). The real crunch for the textile industry, however, occurred after the Second World War. While temporarily revived by war commissions, employment in textile industries in New England dropped from 280,000 in 1947 to 170,000 in 1954 and to 99,000 in 1964 (Eisenmenger, 1967:9).

The Region after World War II

Despite the collapse of New England's textile and shoe industries during the 1930s, in 1940, two out of five employed people were still either working in textile, shoe, or paper industries (Harrison, 1982:1). Dramatic changes took place after the Second World War when the United States became the center of an increasingly internationalized economic system. The demand for military and scientific equipment changed the area's economy. Taylor's scientific management countered union radicalism and reduced the need for highly skilled workers, transforming the productive base from mill-based consumer goods to parts for jet engines and computer hardware and software, and the growing service industries of education and medical care. The flight of small businesses trying to find more favorable climates and corporations branching out of the region contributed to a wave of plant closings.[9] For textile manufacturers in particular, the radicalism of the labor movements, born in the nineteenth century and in full maturity in the 1930s, provided the basis for a class struggle that initiated the historical trend of corporate moves to areas with "better business climates."

Although women played a prominent role in industry in the nineteenth century in New England, their entry into the world of white-collar work after the war resulted in a further lowering of their wages. After World War II, women office workers in New England manufacturing firms earned below the national average and even "below those prevailing in Southern States" (Harrison, 1982:14).

Trade Union Erosion

The restructuring of industry affected trade union organization. Bouyed by governmental policies during the Cold War that weakened the unions and by the relocation of industries, New England business owners were able to describe their workforces as "cooperative" by the 1950s (Eisenmenger, 1967). While in 1950 unions in New England succeeded in organizing 70 percent of the shops they entered, by the 1970s that rate had been reduced to 50 percent, well below other parts of the country (Harrison, 1978:53).

This decline of successful union activity occurred despite their success in improving the relations of work. The effects of union organizing improved the conditions for those still employed in the major manufacturing industries. In Pittsfield, we asked one retired worker in the GE plant to describe his entry into the union and the long-term changes the union produced:

> I worked as a winder in the General Electric Company from 1926 until 1970. I worked for part of that as an apprentice. I started as an apprentice. I was going to become a draftsman but I couldn't draw a picture of anything so they told me that I had to make a change from that and go to something else. So I left and went down to Columbus Avenue and worked there for two years and them I came into the main plant. . . .
>
> In the beginning, there were no unions. But, I was lucky that the man who was my general foreman was also my neighbor, and I could do things that other people in that department couldn't do. They use to tell me "You can't talk to that person on the machine next to you," when I first went in there. But I said ,"The hell I can't, I'm going to," and I did. And the fellow would say, "Go back to your machine. Don't get me in trouble." But then they started to

see that I wasn't worried about anybody getting into trouble and nobody was getting into trouble. . . . And then the UE came in, the organizers, and somehow they got ahold of my name, and they came up to the house, and stayed for about an hour. And I said "Yes, I'm interested in unions." I thought it would be something to get people to join up, but I found out that people were more scared then of joining a union then anybody I'd ever seen. That at the mention of "union" their foreman might fire them, that's what they thought. So we had ten of us, we met weekly, we did everything we could. Secretly, myself and Mr. Ross went and organized the winders. We got them all set to take and sign cards. We were going to do it all at once when we did it. Then we'd have somebody . . . if they did something to one of us, they'd be doing it to all of us. So when 1937 came, I said to Mr. Davis, the organizer: "Come on in and sign us up at noon." Then the General Electric Company got ahold of it. . . . I was working under contract myself, because they wanted me to come back and wind and there was only a certain two men who could wind the job they wanted to get out that time, and I says "No." I was working in Plastics, the dirtiest job in General Electric, but they told me they'd like to have me stay there because they thought they could use a man like me. So when I went back, the superintendent, my foreman, said, "You're coming back to wind," and I said, "No, I'm not," He said, "Well Bus, somebody's got to wind these transformers." I said, "Well, I'm not going to." . . . So then he got the superintendent, Mr. Hubb, and he said that if I didn't come back I would never work in the GE again.

I said, "That's what you say, but your counterpart in the Plastics Department says that I've got a job there as long as I want it, and you've got to fight that out with him." So then they got the manufacturing engineer up there, and he wanted to know why. I said, "Hell, I'll come back here and work for five weeks and get laid off again and be on the streets." I said, "Over there I get 36 hours a week, a minimum of 80 cents an hour." And he said, "Why did you fire him?" And he said, "I had to lay him off because he's not married, he's got no dependents."

In them days that was the thing that they based it on, whether you were married and how many dependents you had, they didn't base it on your service or anything like that, because I had eight years seniority at the time. And I was quite an example for some of the younger people.

So anyway, Mr. Young said, "We will give you a minimum of 80 cents and hour, 36 hours a week, guarantee it to you, if you will take and come back here and wind. He said, "the only thing is . . . if there's no work in winding, you'll have to go all over the department and work there where ever we think we can use you.' I said, "I'll take it." So I took and worked with that until the morning when I was going to sign up all the guys and they caught me.

They said, "you're going to join a union?" I says, "yes." They said, "What are you joining a union for? You've got everything you want anyway." I said, "That's just one individual. But wait until I get 5000 people behind me and then see what I'll do."

So that was the start. The winders all signed up at noon. I lost my guarantee. I started to work three days a week, one week off every four. That's the way it went . . . until the War broke out. Then they needed everybody.

When asked about the decline in union membership, he responded:

I think the union improved conditions of the employees at least 10,000 percent, that's the way I look at it. People were free and everything like that. They had coffee breaks. We never had a coffee break. We never knew what it was. I never had a coffee break until five or six years before I retired. Then I began to see that they were getting a coffee break. They certainly negotiate a lot better pensions today than we went out under . . . people take unions for granted and they think that the conditions are there and that they don't have to pay somebody to get those same conditions.

This union leader's recollection of the days of union organizing and his comparison to current conditions are local and specific. As with many of the union and nonunion workers in the General Electric plant, the existing conditions are assumed rather than attributed to specific struggles that took place during the decades of the twentieth century. The ideological level at which management is able to convert entitlements won in union struggles to benefits provided by the corporation presents screens to those who have not directly experienced the struggle. There are, of course, union members who are aware of the mystification that takes place and who remain dedicated to the education of plant members. Ironically, many of the younger workers in the region are from families who were participants in these struggles. The discipline and work ethic that is passed down through generations benefited the corporation, while the system of "negotiated class struggle" acted to hold down formal confrontations between management and labor.[10]

Notes on the Service Sector

The service sector is the fastest-growing area of the economy in New England. From the 1950s, it has shown the greatest amount of growth in employment. Along with the service sector, the New England Economy Project found five consequent propositions about the "new" New England economy, drawn from the U.S. Social Security Administration's Longitudinal Employer-Employee Analyses Data File (LEED):[11]

- Wage levels have fallen, relative to other regions (including the South) and especially in terms of purchasing power. This is true even for people who work year round, and for skilled systems analysts as well as for factory workers.
- Earned income is becoming more unequally distributed among the region's workers over time, both between and within (most) industries, even among those who work year round, and within as well as between the sexes.
- Employment in the region is highly unstable in several respects: There is a growing incidence of part-time or part-year jobs; the degree of employee attachment to the companies for which they work is lowest in precisely those industries which are growing most rapidly; service-intensive regional economies such as New England have shown themselves not to be recession-proof (as was widely believed); and the region's highest-paying manufacturing companies —the aircraft and metalworking industries—are subject to sharp "boom-bust" swings in employment.
- There are significant barriers to upward mobility for many of the region's workers, including those who were employed at one time in the old mill industries, and women and minorities employed in the service sector.
- The developmental tendencies toward rationalization and geographic restructuring, which underlay the erosion of the old economic base of the region, are still operative, even in the most rapidly growing industries.

Between 1973 and 1977, real wages dropped sharply in New England relative to the country as a whole (Browne, 1980:44, quoted in Harrison, 1981:71).

The data presents dramatic effects on the population. Many of the workers employed by the mills were not able to transfer their skills to the new manufacturing, service, or "high tech" industries. Of the 833,000 employed by mill industries in 1958, 674,000 left mill employment. In 1975 only 18,000 of this cohort was employed in the high-tech industries of the region (Harrison, 1981:89).[12]

Philosophers of "post industrial society" have contended that the growth of the service sector is an inevitable part of economic growth and beneficial to the hiring of sectors traditionally discriminated against in the labor market. The growth of this sector shows that fragmentation of tasks, the deskilling of work and job insecurity are not dependent on collar color or on gender. Service sector jobs are more likely to pay lower wages and provide inadequate hours for heads of households. Once believed recession-proof, the New England Economy Project found that regional economies built on service industries are just as likely to experience downturns as others based primarily on manufacturing. Further, facilitating union service section economies act to diminish erosion, social and community life. In short, the growth of the service sector has had a negative impact on communities, particularly in Pittsfield.

CHAPTER 5

The Pittsfield Community

The restructuring of industry and the devaluation of the community by its major corporation has residents scrambling as they attempt to adapt to changing circumstances. The willingness of many residents and smaller industries to remain committed testifies to the strength of organizations and the involvement of its residents in the hope for the region.

Early Industry in Pittsfield

Early industry in Pittsfield is synonymous with the growth of mills in America. The Pittsfield textile industry predates most of New England's. Unlike the town's counterparts in the eastern part of the state, local entrepreneurs originally capitalized most of the mills. With the area's isolation and independent spirit, fostered by the mountain ranges that split the state, and culminating in the Stockbridge Convention in 1774 that urged the "nonconsumption of British goods," local manufacturers established themselves despite the superior position of postcolonial trade in the east.

The early mills in Pittsfield relied on water power, controlled by the city fathers.[1] The earliest mill dates to 1801, established by the entrepreneur Arthur Schofield. The War of 1812 brought orders for blankets, uniforms, and sails from the United States Army and for iron goods in the developing industry of iron forging. The end of the war threatened these plants as cheaper and better-quality cloth became available from England. Succeeding in their campaign for a tariff law, the mills continued to prosper until their slow demise in the twentieth century.

Pittsfield by 1800 was the largest town in western Massachusetts, with 2,261 registered residents. By 1875, it had a population of 12,267, more than five times than that of its closest neighbors. Textile manufacturing, however, was not the only industry. Manufactured goods included paper, metal, shoes, and saddles. Farming was still an important component of the economy.

While the mills in Berkshire County were founded independently from the rest of the state, local industry was not immune from the relations of production that dominated wool and cotton production at the time. Pittsfield's employers, though, were noted for their ability to encourage and retain long-term employees. William Smith in his early history of Pittsfield (1876), for example, commends the early mill owner William Pomeroy for maintaining a stable workforce, writing that "A peculiarity in the management of the Pomeroy Mills, which they share with that of other old Pittsfield factories, is the long retention of faithful employees" (Smith, 1876:479). The demand for cheaper labor and competition from mills in other parts of New England eventually led to the decline of older firms at the end of the nineteenth century. Employment and capitalization fluctuated in all parts of the state, with what Smith called "acts of God," meaning the changes in consumption that reduced production and produced unemployment. Industry was uneven and the consumer market not yet stable as a driving force in productive relations. Workers who lived in North Adams, for example, enjoyed a high level of employment even during the depression years of the 1890s, with the Arnold Mills of North Adams making a popular brand of stuffed toy dogs and cats (Keyssar, 1986:119). Though there are no accurate statistics on unemployment in Pittsfield in those years, cycles of unemployment were frequent. As the labor process transformed the rest of New England after the Civil War, so it was in Pittsfield. The consolidation of capital and the increase in capital-intensive production changed the nature of industry in the area.[2]

Still, the growth of the city was fueled by the immigration of Italians, Poles, and French Canadians. Like other areas of New England, these waves of immigration created ethnic divisions and competition over work, preventing the labor force from forging a unified response to exploitation in the relations of industrial work. Immigrants were viewed as primitives willing to perform any task, and they were willing to travel. One writer of Pittsfield history tells us that the Italians, who dominated the workforce in the early 1900s, "were a wandering tribe of people in those days . . . going wherever work invited. They were content to camp in open fields or deserted buildings on the outskirts of the City, cooking for themselves, gypsy fashion; sleeping on hay or rough blankets spread upon the ground after their day's hard work in ditches, or climbing ladders under the burden of mortar boards, and the heat of boiling sun rays" (Mullany, 1924:vii). These immigrants brought with them traditions that bound them as a community but estranged them from the settled generations before them:

> We all remember them flocking into town with their household
> belongings draped upon their backs, and all their other earthly

goods in the roped black boxes carried in their hands; a nomad race, despised and suspected. . . . They brought with them habits of settling disputes that have prevailed in their country for ages—as the code of honor, and these horrified us, naturally. They wrangled among themselves, and knives were in evidence at once—sometimes with fatal results—but not often. The wounded, however, barely escaped death, more frequently than we like to relate. This vengeful characteristic of a quick-tempered Sicilian who formed the majority of these laborers gangs, make them a dreaded people everywhere, which is but natural. (Mullany, 1924:vii)

Pittsfield, like Cumbler's (1979) description of Lynn, Massachusetts, was, in the end, able to incorporate the immigrants into the locale with little disruption. Unlike areas such as Fall River, where mass waves of immigrants resulted in considerable clashes, Pittsfield's residents forged a cohesive community able to live and work together.[3]

General Electric and the Growth of a Company Town

By 1895 Pittsfield had a diversified industrial base. The Massachusetts census of manufacturers listed 200 private firms and 21 corporations. The fastest-growing industry, with four firms, was electrical manufacturing. A major wave of industrial change took place in the late nineteenth and early twentieth century as electrical machinery production took hold. Railroad transportation created a national market and corporate takeovers absorbed small firms and intensified the capitalization of industry (Tractenberg, 1982; Nash, 1989). In Pittsfield, William Stanley ventured into electrical machinery in 1887, inventing the first polyphase alternating-current generator.

The success of Stanley's operation and the need for further capitalization stimulated more takeovers, and General Electric purchased Stanley's plant in 1903. No longer a local industrial concern, when confronted with worker dissatisfaction GE threatened to close the plant and "disemploy" the 1,500 trained workers it inherited. The profitable market for power transformers, however, made continuation of the product line desirable, militating against overzealous corporate moves against its workers.

Labor unrest was prominent in Pittsfield during the early part of the twentieth century. But the unions faced a formidable opponent in General Electric. A major strike in 1916 intensified the division between management and labor, solidifying the relations of power that would come to dominate labor relations for the next century. With several production plants to which it could shift production, General Electric yielded considerable authority over the workers and even state agencies. Strikebreakers were protected by police paid for at public expense, and workers in other plants, worried about their own security, did not ally with their cohorts.

With the general decline of the textile industry during the 1920s and 1930s, General Electric dominated employment, providing Pittsfield's major tax base. The Second World War provided major funding as the federal government created the Defense Plant Corporation and publicly financed General Electric's ordnance plant in Pittsfield, as well as others in Lynn and Everett (Harrison, 1982:27).[4]

Assuming the role of the primary industry in the area, General Electric kept out other industry and maintained a tight control over a highly skilled labor force. Its dominance allowed it to maintain the upper hand in the "negotiated class struggle" of the twentieth century. Workers did, despite the obstacles, win major concessions from General Electric during major strikes in 1916, 1946, and 1969. The 1969 strike, however, marked a decline of union power, fueled by increasing threats by the corporation to relocate production.

The industrial restructuring that took place during the 1830s, at the beginning of the twentieth century, and after the Second World War, is again taking place in Pittsfield.

Industrial Decline and the Issue of Development

The extent of the effect of restructuring on Pittsfield is well documented by both local and state agencies. The Pittsfield Economic Revitalization Corporation (PERC) produced the most comprehensive report, introducing its *Economic Base Study of Pittsfield and Berkshire County* by stating that:

> Pittsfield and Berkshire County are experiencing a fundamental change that will affect the social and economic life of the region. Manufacturing, which provided the foundation of the region's economy, is in a state of serious decline. How the region responds to this change will determine the area's economic health into the next century. (PERC, 1988:1)

Summarizing the trends in the economy and its effect on residents, the report goes on to say that

> Changes in new employment and opportunities caused both wealth and poverty to increase. On one hand, wealth increased with the rapid increase in high tech and professional jobs. On the other hand, the rapid increase in low-paying service and retail jobs has caused an increase in the number of working poor. As the rate of economic change increased many workers lost jobs in what had been considered secure occupations and in effect fell out of the

middle class. These economic circumstances have combined to create a large group of single mothers, young people, and displaced blue collar workers for whom there is little hope for achieving a middle-class lifestyle. (PERC, 1988:1)

Moreover, the report continues, Bureau of the Census statistics indicate that

First, the increase in retail activity has partly been due to federal tax cuts and lower energy costs resulting in increased disposable income. The increases in housing costs have been largely due to the decrease in interest rates, the increase in the number of households, the demand for second houses, and the short-term build-up of employment at G.E.'s Ordinance Systems. The unemployment rate has declined in recent years but this can be attributed to a decline in the size of the labor force. *The best indication of economic health is population migration. In the case of Pittsfield and Berkshire County, the population trends indicate that this region is failing to provide adequate opportunities for its citizens.* (PERC, 1988:2, emphasis added).

At the time of the distribution of the PERC report, General Electric announced projected layoffs at its Ordinance Systems. Speculating that the federal government would tailor defense spending, managers planned for the layoff of approximately 500 workers to adjust to the assumed cut in defense spending that produced the "Massachusetts Miracle."[5]

Community Effects of Economic Restructuring

The Office of the Massachusetts Division of Employment Security provides to the state's communities detailed records of trends in the labor and manufacturing market. *The Annual Planning Information Report for the Fiscal Year 1982* reported that Pittsfield peaked in 1980, and predicted that the reliance on one major manufacturer would result in a continued "slippage" in the economy (1982:1). The General Electric Corporation terminated 3,000 jobs between 1974 and 1982, which the planning report states were "due to the energy price escalation, which has produced less demand for power transformers, the expiration of defense contracts, and appropriation cuts that affect ordnance" (1982:2).

As a result of these changes, the population dropped from 57,000 to 52,000 between 1970 and 1980, and from 52,000 to 49,000 between 1980 and 1990. Statistics on population trends have the population further dropping to 45,000 by the year 2,010 (see table 5.1). The largest decline among those under twenty and the largest increase in population among unrelated

Table 5.1. Population Trends

	Persons	*% change*
1980	51,974	
1990	48,622	–6.5
2000	47,463	–2.4
2010	45,267	–4.6

Persons by Sex (1990 U.S. Census)
Male	23,091
Female	25,531

Age Distribution (1990 U.S. Census)

Persons		%
Under 5	3,345	6.9
5–14	5,879	12.1
15–44	21,425	44.1
45–64	9,585	19.7
65 & over	8,388	17.3

Source: Regional Planning Agency, Department of Housing and Community Development.

Table 5.2. Households (1990 U.S. Census)

1980	*1990*	*% change*
19,436	19,916	+2.5

Household Size (1990 US Census)
2.41 persons per household

Households by Type (1990 US Census)

Households		%
Married Couple Family	9,930	49.9
Male Householder	614	3.1
Female Householder	2,528	12.7
Nonfamily Household	6,844	34.4

Source: 1990 U.S. Census and the Regional Planning Agency, Department of Housing and Community Development.

Table 5.3. Housing

	Housing Units	%
Total Units	21,272	
Total Occupied	19,916	
owner occupied	11,862	59.6
renter occupied	8,054	40.4
Total vacant	1,356	
for sale	168	12.4
for rent	592	43.7
other vacant	596	44.0
Owner Vacancy Rate		1.4
Rental Vacancy Rate		6.8
Median Value (owner occupied)	$111,100	
Rent (renter occupied)	$388	

Source: 1990 U.S. Census and the Regional Planning Agency, Department of Housing and Community Development.
Note: Value is the Census respondent's estimate of how much the property, including lot, would sell for if it were for sale.

households (table 5.2). Vacancy rates reflect outmigration, while housing costs shows the bifurcation of the labor force and the depression of the region. Housing starts are slow. Almost half of Pittsfield's housing was built before 1940 (tables 5.3 and 5.4). The fertility rate dropped by 18 percent. Young people were leaving Pittsfield.

By all indications the economic forecast for the city of Pittsfield is grim. Three thousand more manufacturing jobs disappeared in Berkshire County between 1984 and 1987, a loss of over 10 percent of income in basic employment (PERC, 1988:37). The labor force decreased by more than 2,268 members from 1984 to 1986, indicating that working age members of the community are leaving the area (see table 5.5). The Pittsfield Economic Revitalization Corporation's report concluded that an increase in labor force participation by Pittsfield's residents, despite the decline in the labor force, indicated an even larger decline in the population. The report predicted an even larger out-migration as manufacturing jobs continue to decrease (tables 5.6 and 5.7).

The most frequently cited reason for Pittsfield's industrial decline is the high cost of labor, contrasting with the general lowering of labor costs across the United States. The major cited change in costs relative to the United States in Pittsfield included the transportation of goods. Although taxes are often cited as a problem, Pittsfield does not have higher taxes than other regions, and taxes are not a large part of U.S. corporation cost structures.

Table 5.4. Housing Structures

Type of Structure (1990 U.S. Census)	Units	%
Single units	11,311	53.2
2-4 units	6,501	30.6
5 or more units	3,064	14.4
Other	396	1.9
Year Structure Built (1990 US Census)	*Units*	*%*
1989-March 1990	157	0.7
1980-1988	1,639	7.7
1970-1979	1,920	9.0
1960-1969	2,140	10.1
1950-1959	2,485	11.7
1940-1949	2,329	10.9
1939 or earlier	6024	9.8
Home Sales (Banker and Tradesman)	*Number*	*% change*
1990	524	-34.4
1991	495	-5.5
1992	590	19.2
1993	654	11.2
1994	648	-0.9
Median Sales (Banker and Tradesman)	*Price*	*% change*
1990	106,400	-1.0
1991	96,000	-9.8
1992	90,000	-6.3
1993	84,000	-6.7
1994	85,000	1.2

Source: 1990 U.S. Census and the Regional Planning Agency, Department of Housing and Community Development.

Note: Home Sales and Home Prices: Data for all transactions between $25,000 and $1,000,000. Condominium sales and prices are included.

Table 5.5. Labor Force (1990 U.S. Census)

Employed	22,379
Unemployed	1,835
Unemployment Rate	7.6%
statewide	6.7%
Industry Groups of Residents (1990 U.S. Census)	
Agriculture	135
Mining	23
Construction	1,486
Manufacturing	4,749
Transportation anc communication	1,071
Wholesale and retail trade	5,242
Finance, Insurance and real estate	1,275
Government	711
Services	7,687
Total	22,379

Source: 1990 U.S. Census and the Regional Planning Agency, Department of Housing and Community Development.

Table 5.6. Employment, Payroll, and Sales: Average Annual Employment by Place of Work

Agriculture	85
Mining	C
Construction	850
Manufacturing	4,637
Transportation & Communication	921
Wholesale & Retail Trade	5,273
Finance, Insurance & Real Estate	1,497
Government	2,391
Services	9,192
Total	24,862
Total Annual Payroll ($000) 686,572	
Average Annual Wage ($) 27,615	
Number of Establishments 1,392	

Source: Department of Employment and Training and Regional Planning Agency, Commonwealth of Massachusetts, 1993.

Employment and Wages: Data for employment and wages covered by unemployment compensation. Data is confidential (identified with a "C") if there are less than three reporting units in the total, or if one unit accounts for 80% or more of the total. Reporting problems of multilocation employers may result in some over- or underreporting.

Table 5.7. Income Distribution (1990 U.S. Census)

	Households	*%*
Less than $5,000	788	4.0
$5,000–$9,999	2,394	12.0
$10,000–$24,999	5,212	26.2
$25,000–$34,999	3,207	16.1
$35,000–$49,999	3,541	17.8
$50,000–$74,999	3,437	17.3
$75-000–$99,999	850	4.3
$100,000 or more	672	3.4
Median household income $29,987		
State rank		310
% of state average		81.2%
Per capita income		$15,426
State rank		226
% of state average		89.6%

Source: 1990 U.S. Census and the Regional Planning Agency, Department of Housing and Community Development.

Table 5.8. Sources of Income (1990 U.S. Census)

	Number of Households	*Average Income*
Wage and salary	14,475	$38,061
Nonfarm self-employed	1,753	16,361
Farm self-employed	86	11,073
Social Security	6,749	7,780
Public assistance	2,119	4,911
Retirement	4,423	8,408
Interest	9,392	5,661
Other	2,701	4,258

Source: 1990 U.S. Census and the Regional Planning Agency, Department of Housing and Community Development.

Likewise, energy costs, which are also frequently cited as a problem for Pittsfield, are not major cost factors. Unlike the nineteenth century when companies imported labor to lower wages, corporations now transfer technology and even whole physical plants to other American regions and overseas, seeking out cheaper labor while increasing transportation costs for consumption of the products in the primary markets. While citing the need for skilled labor, companies have long complained about the costs of labor in the area.

A major consequence of the loss of manufacturing jobs and the consequent lowering of wages is out-migration. The Pittsfield Economic Revitalization Corporation cited this trend as a factor in the diminishing labor pool:

> Labor costs are often the most important factor in siting decisions. Traditionally Berkshire County has had higher than average manufacturing wages and lower than average wages in all other sectors. Manufacturing wages have been high because of the dominant place of G.E. and other large unionized shops in the local economy. The downward trend in manufacturing employment should eventually place downward pressure on wages.
>
> This process is hindered when unemployed workers leave the area. Recent large increases in housing costs have priced some low wage earners out of the housing market. It is the exit of these workers from the area more than an increase in jobs that has kept the regional unemployment rate low. The lack of available workers in the low wage category is hurting the service and retail industries as well as making the area less attractive for industrial expansion. (PERC, 1988:41).

The study indicates the workers "are sensitive to living cost in much the same way industries are sensitive to labor costs" (PERC, 1988:41). But it fails to distinguish the relationship between the two categories. Out-migration takes place as members of the labor force seek perceived available jobs in other regions. This out-migration has produced a shift in the population, particularly in the loss of males between the age of 15 and 65, with females taking up some of the slack in labor for lower-paid jobs and increasing the gap in wage levels between men and women.

For those who chose to stay in the area, a widening gap developed between the rich and the poor, and for most, the standard of living declined.

Between 1970 and 1980, real wages fell by 15 percent in the area. During the same period, family poverty increased 108 percent, with the largest increase in female-headed households (PERC, 1988:11). The strain of unemployment and economic decline shows most profoundly in the doubling of the divorce rate between 1970 and 1980.

Even when they were able to keep their jobs, Pittsfield's workers showed stress. Many of the employed workers whom we interviewed in 1982 worked overtime, leaving little time for their families or leisure. At the same time that these individuals were accumulating overtime, however, the management at GE was busily planning and implementing layoffs. The seeming contradiction is management economics: less employment means less capital outlay for benefits, while at the same time planning for production can be performed on an ad-hoc basis. The irony of this policy is not lost on the community: as one laid-off worker commented: "I think it's all goofed up. They want to lay off a lot of people and those who remain work harder."

The majority of the workers we interviewed were connected to General Electric through family. One or both of their parents had worked in the plant and many of them had siblings in the plant. None were optimistic about the future of the corporation in the community. The effects of economic decline in Pittsfield are mediated by a tradition of self-help and a domestic orientation. A history of a strong kin-based community and the experience of union activities have forged bonds, acting to provide assistance both inside and outside the family. While Paul and Wallace (1985) document that more sharing of household and community labor takes place among *employed* workers, our interviews noted that a substantial amount of shared work was performed by unemployed workers on family members' and friend's houses, businesses and cars[6]. When asked about daily activities, one unmarried laid-off worker responded:

> Sometimes I get up early, sometimes I'll sleep till 10, 11 o'clock, I got an old jeep down the garage, I go out in it once or twice a week, my brother had an old station wagon, I just fixed that for him last week, my other brothers got an engine I'm rebuilding for his car. Fairly good at cars. What I do for a career, getting dirty all the time, once in a while I don't mind what we were doing today, cutting up some fire wood, cleaning out the garage last week, cleaning out the basement yesterday. I got a friend who waxes cars for a living, he's got a small business, so once in a while he gets a car, maybe once or twice a week I go down and help him, sit around alot.

Voluntary Associations, Community Organization, and Corporate Morality

Voluntary organizations in late capitalism have come to play the dominant role in maintaining community viability, acting as buffers against economic decline in the same way that families, kin groups, and unions did in the nineteenth century.

Pittsfield has an active roster of community organizations ranging from the Boys Club to the United Way, and community organizations such as General Electric's "Athletic Club" that serves workers from the plant. In the early days of industrialization, it was the families that owned the mills who made the major contributions that kept the organizations alive. The Crane family, owners of the paper mill that produces United States currency and fine stationary, endowed the Boys Club, still one of the largest in the country. In 1968, the Boys Club launched a fund raising effort that produced 1.5 million in ten weeks. Still, the boards of the Boys Club, the United Way, the YMCA and YWCA, and other community organizations reads like an elite list culled from GE and the other major industries in the area. Particularly in periods of economic growth, it is important for the corporation to maintain the viability of labor reproduction through community organizations. With the family unit declining as the primary socializing mechanism for workers, other institutions, such as schools, hospitals, and clinics become paramount in training the future workforce, and when their health is diminished, their productive capacity becomes compromised (Gintis and Bolwes, 1976).

General Electric's lessened presence to the city appears clearly in its reduced participation in community events such as the Halloween and the Fourth of July parades, where the size of its floats seem directly correlated to its disinvestment in major production. Even the corporation's participation in community fund drives became perfunctory as its relationship with the community deteriorated and its interest in the labor force waned. The community responded to these developments by increasing its already substantial participation in organizational efforts. The United Way drive in 1982 was one of the most successful of its history, despite GE's decreased organizational participation. The use of voluntary associations to solidify community relations in periods of economic downturn softens the blow of the depression taking place.

The corporation planned its involvement with and support of the community on its own terms. When John F. Welch, a Pittsfield resident, became General Electric's chief executive officer, he terminated 100,000 employees and determined that each of the corporation's businesses had to be first or second in its market to keep from being "shuttered." As *Fortune* reported in 1986, "In five years General Electric's perpetual motion boss has chopped 100,000 jobs, sunk billions of dollars in automated factories, overhauled the corporate culture, and picked up RCA in the costliest non-oil merger ever. He promises still more to come." Welch's actions have labeled him "neutron Jack." Producing a statement of corporate values, he suggested that managers who did not agree should find other avenues for employment. This statement, of course, reflects more than a simple change in corporate structure. Corporate culture does not exist in a vacuum, but instead reflects the dominant ideologies of the power elite (Nash and Kirsch, 1987). Media attempts to personalize corporate changes reify the personality of the individual spokespeople while all but ignoring the consequences of corporate restructuring (see, for example, *Fortune*, July 7, 1987; *Business Week*, June 30, 1986).

For Pittsfield, the ideology of the corporation has had a devastating effect. The corporation's history of core manufacturing in power transformers predicted future changes that were to take place. In a tradition that does justice to Bourdieu's (1977) notion of "symbolic violence," the corporation's statements throughout the decade of the 1980s were filled with quotes from Welch about his love for the area and his commitment to the community. The Power Transformer division closed in 1987. In good public relations fashion, the face of the corporation was that of a "responsible" corporate citizen: explaining to the community that it would try to keep production going but making it aware that profits had to be made if the company was to survive in the present economy.

Clearly keeping up the image of the caring company while cutting back on production takes its toll even on highly skilled public relations personnel. One community relations manager told us during an interview in 1982 that GE could simply not play the role of "Daddy Warbucks" anymore. This pattern of giving priority to profits regardless of human costs has become the core of an amoral "modus operandi" of corporate planning. It is a cost-accounting approach that has influenced American cultural values and has even gained scientific credibility.

The Corporation and the Community

Merry (1986) suggests that at least two kinds of ideology need to be addressed in the "negotiated, constructed reality developed in local social settings" (1986:255). The first is a "top-down elite-produced and disseminated ideology" and the second a "bottom-up, locally constructed one." She suggests that the coexistence of these needs produces an ideological pluralism "in the same way that subcultures are plural in complex societies." What she misses is the facets of power that determine the adoption of ideologies for economic purposes, the "things are as I say they are" that Wolf (1985) borrows from *Alice in Wonderland* to describe the sociopolitical domain of power relations.

The cultural values of Pittsfield's residents, emphasizing marriage, the family, and property are symbolic aspects of the community and lie at the foundations of its survival. Interviews with residents suggest a provisional base for David Schneider's (1968) *American Kinship* categories. Family and kinship in Pittsfield represent how aspects of an individual's life *should* be conducted; they need not have any basis in empirical reality. That these values exist unites families and kinship groups responding to threats from the outside even as its internal dynamics are being destroyed. Families want to stay in Pittsfield because of its binding cultural values. Small companies want to stay in the area for the same reasons, aware that their businesses would do better elsewhere but determined to maintain a lifestyle to which they and their employees have aspired. This seeming contradiction in business logic provides an answer to Eisenmeyer's (1967) query as to why a majority of executives chose to stay in New England despite its "locational disadvantages."

CHAPTER 6

Development Strategies

The flight of capital and the physical movement of corporate facilities in the United States have destabilized economic relationships that had been in place since the turn of the century (Yago, 1983:115). These changes have altered geopolitical trade relationships, resulting in profound structural changes on the local level. Particularly in cities where a multinational corporation dominates the economy, changes in world trade relationships have led to a schism between corporate and community cycles in the name of competitive advantage. The result is often the creation of a leadership vacuum in the attempts at economic development planning. As one city official confided in 1987, "We're a community that's running around with blinders on poking around in the dark trying to figure out where we're going. We don't have the base information we need to know what's happening."

As localities confront the restructuring of industry, the concept of "development" takes on new meaning for the rebuilding of destabilized communities. The term itself has taken on mystical proportions, signifying *a solution*. New development is understood by community leaders as an increase in economic growth and an increase in the redistribution of capital. But the optimism associated with development planning disappears when consensus becomes difficult to achieve and the magnitude of competing interests is realized. This process has proved chaotic in Pittsfield.

Defining Development

The primary objective of development planning in capitalist societies is the social and political stability necessary for private sector investment. In cities such as Pittsfield where a single dominant investor exists, and where "labor" and "management" are viable categories, the secondary role of government agencies in relation to private industry is pronounced. Outright signs of class struggle are not evident in Pittsfield, but the confusion and ambivalence toward the development process are an expression of differing class interests and orientations. The emphasis on the necessity of "changing local attitudes" put forward by business interests and parroted by government officials is a response to the social and political restructuring required for increased capital accumulation. This ambivalence, and the attempts to tame it, resulted in a crisis of management in Pittsfield.

Discussion of development in Pittsfield takes place in the realm of local definitions that differ for those with a "native" point of view and for others without a long residence history. It is measured by the criteria important to the sector, defining the phenomena and the relationships of dependency that permeate the discussion.

The primary sectors in the public discussion of development are the family, the community, city government, industry, and tourism. While the interests of these sectors may overlap, their positions in the schema of "development" are often at odds. Families are concerned about housing costs and valuation, jobs and security for present and future generations. These concerns have become particularly prominent in Pittsfield as the children of long-term workers at the General Electric plant follow the promise of jobs to other regions of the country. The contradiction presented by a tourist trade that is raising land and home values and a declining industrial base that is lowering real income causes a tension that is expressed in discussions of strategy.

The family is still strong in Pittsfield. Goody's (1978) contention that the family has been dismantled under industrial capitalism may hold true as a unit of consumption, but it still acts as a unit seeking to preserve continuity in rapidly changing circumstances. The community as a viable entity is composed of kinship networks and the services that sustain them. The history and continuity of the community is particularly strong. For generations there was stable employment. Even in the current crisis, the community remains a strong entity supporting voluntary organizations and fund-raising efforts. Organized labor serves as a means for community identification. One of the prime concerns of worker's organizations is the trend toward the weakening of the labor movement as national and international economic trends strengthen the position of those with capital mobility and control. While labor is necessarily pro-development, it cannot be so at the expense of its own membership and community base.

City managers are involved with the maintenance of a tax base that can sustain the infrastructure of the community. They are confronted with all of the conflicting relationships that define the phenomenon of economic development and are placed in the precarious position of negotiating the lines between family, business, industry, and the need for revenue. The differing standards has generated a development schizophrenia where strategic positions are shuffled daily and the city's position is in continual motion. The difficulty of defining development strategies resulted in a high turnover for economic development officers who were thwarted in their efforts by changing allegiances and actions by the competing sectors.

Planning for industrial development in Pittsfield is conditioned by the history of the largest corporation and its relationship with the community. General Electric has been in control of Pittsfield's development since its takeover of the Stanley works in 1904, and its policies are determined by corporate headquarters outside of the city. The growth in the service sector now overruns manufacturing, providing lower-paying employment for members of a skilled labor force. Finally, tourism has become the fastest-growing segment of the economy in Pittsfield. Although local business are buoyed by the purchasing power of visiting New Yorkers and Bostonians, there is widespread apprehension about the ability of the tourist trade to compensate for the declining manufacturing sector, and about the effect of increased population and development pressures on the environment.

Development Agencies

For a community of fifty thousand, Pittsfield has an impressive array of agencies and committees responsible for development issues. The mayor's Office of Community and Economic Development is the primary arm of city government addressing these concerns and it interacts with others established by private business, the Chamber of Commerce, and research institutes. Along with the Office of Community and Economic Development, there is the Pittsfield Economic Revitalization Corporation, which in 1988 produced the most comprehensive report on the city, the Berkshire County Regional Planning Commission, the Central Berkshire Chamber of Commerce, the Commercial Area Revitalization District Board, the Pittsfield Housing Authority (which designates developers for a large area of the downtown tract), the Berkshire Development Council, the now defunct Berkshire County Development Commission, and the Massachusetts Division of Employment Security, which maintains a research division for planning purposes and outside agencies producing reports, such as the John F. Kennedy School of Government at Harvard. These agencies and sources have, in the 1990s, been joined by The Berkshire County Revitalization Corporation, the Pittsfield Airport Commissioners, the Corporation for Central Berkshire, and the Downtown Development Corporation. The *Berkshire Eagle* produces an annual report on the region's business and industry, and many of the commissions and agencies listed above have subcommittees. These agencies and committees do not represent specific interest groups. The major division in development planning is between "native" approaches to the problem and those of "outside" consultants and developers.

Development Perspectives: Reports in Search of Problem Definition

The General Electric Corporation's reduced role in community and economic development during the late sixties and early seventies produced a crisis of management that has lasted until the present day. It took almost a decade before the realities of the leadership crisis took hold and the city began its spate of development activities. These efforts include reports and planning documents that agree in content but lack concrete political analyses of the current scene. The first major report on the Berkshire economy was prepared in June of 1981 by the Regional Science Research Institute in Amherst, Massachusetts. *The Berkshire County Economy: Problems, Potentials and Transportation Implications* was produced under the auspices of the Berkshire County Regional Planning Commission, with help from Williams College and funding from the U.S. Department of Transportation. The introduction tells us that

> The study for which this is the final report was undertaken in response to the concern of the Berkshire County Regional Planning Commission, and other public and private groups and agencies, caused by the apparent stagnation of the County's economy. The slow growth evidenced in the late 1970's and the potential problems inherent in the population decline, as indicated by the preliminary 1980 Census figures, suggest that more vigorous public and private efforts may be needed to insure that sufficient numbers of jobs at decent wages will be available to the County's residents in future years.

Anxiety about the county's economic future has been precipitated especially by the cutback of employment at the power transformer division of General Electric during the mid-seventies. This cutback could have led to higher levels of unemployment in the county, had it not been for *(a)* the out-migration of some of the skilled General Electric workers (and their families) whose jobs were eliminated and *(b)* some growth in nondurable good manufacturing. The other mitigating factor appears to have been an upsurge in trade and service employment associated, in part, with rapid growth in the tourist industry.

A later study initiated by the Berkshire County Development Commission and completed by two degree candidates at Harvard's Kennedy School of Government concluded that "*everyone in development has the same goal; to create jobs in a way that does not destroy the beauty of the county* (Calahan and Watson, 1984:5, emphasis in the original), and the report went on to emphasize that

> *the economic development community is very divisive, and coordinated, county-wide development is unworkable.* The county has three separate geographic locations which view development in different ways. The towns view themselves as autonomous and find it very hard to work within the artificial boundaries of a county line. The public and private sectors are often at war with each other and with themselves over development projects. The type of atmosphere does not lend itself to efficient or successful economic development. (Calahan and Watson, 1984:5)

Calahan and Watson's report chastises community leaders for a divisiveness at odds with the major goal, job creation, and warns that the economic scene is worse than perceived:

> a main reason for this fighting is that the towns are just not desperate enough to cooperate. The population and economic decline have been so gradual the county does not feel a sense of crisis. Yet there is cause for alarm. People are leaving at a rate much higher than the national average because they cannot find upwardly mobile types of jobs and the manufacturing base of the county is declining. (Calahan and Watson, 1984:46)

The Production of Chaos

The conclusions of the report were no surprise to those who have been working on economic development. One of the major recommendations, that the Berkshire County Regional Planning Commission play a more active and visible role in economic development, was cut short when the commission was abolished by the city of Pittsfield, a victim of the same fighting over turf that the report pointed to as a major impediment. The report refused to acknowledge that turf is political and that power relationships are inherent pieces of the development puzzle.

The need for the city government to maintain a responsive environment for capitalist accumulation and at the same time manage the political sensitivities of its citizens presents incompatible demands. Friedland, Piven, and Alford (1984) argue that urban governments by necessity separate the economic and the political functions of government in an attempt to mediate contradictory interests.[1] While they argue that this separation succeeds in facilitating the integration of political participants, the effect of the structural separation of the political and economic arenas is less obvious in cities with a strong and organized labor force. Attempts to respond to the needs of the corporation and to the demands of its citizens produces chaos in city planning. The commissioners of economic development, often not informed of deals maneuvered in the mayor's office, are unaware of how their own agendas fit into the city's political structure. The lack of structural coordination between segments of the city bureaucracy is the chief source of the creation for new commissions and committees on development strategies and policies.

The studies and projections differ in format and direction, but they all conclude that the city is in trouble. The *City Report* produced on a yearly basis by the mayor's office is by choice optimistic, concentrating on trends that put prospects for the future in a rosy light. In 1986, then Mayor Smith noted that "Excitement continues to mount as the economy remains strong: Housing starts are above normal, businesses and industry continue to expand and unemployment remains low." The optimism was repeated in 1987, when Smith noted that

> Pittsfield continues to grow and mature. Our priorities are clearer than ever. We have continually strengthened our image and are fast becoming known as America's finest community. The quality of life, the beauty of our lakes and mountains, and the cultural and recreational activities offered here continue to attract new citizens second home owners, and tourists. Our one flaw is not being able to hold our children because of a lack of good employment. (1987 report to the city)

Mayor Smith believed it was necessary to promote a healthy image for the city despite reports to the contrary, including a *New York Times* article suggesting that Pittsfield was the third fastest declining city in the country. There is a belief held by city officials that the town has to be sold on itself. As Mayor Smith told us on the subject of economic development:

> We're doing all the things we can to promote our City and to sell our City. I think one of the toughest things was to sell it to our own people. You know you have a tendency to take things for granted when you live here all your own life. Your take it for granted that it's beautiful here, we have four seasons and beautiful recreation areas and all kinds of things. And after a while you take it for granted and you have to take and promote it to your own people in your community to give them a lift. Oh, we've done all kinds of things. We brought—we've worked very closely since I've been in office with the arts to promote the arts in this City. We were very instrumental in getting Berkshire Public Theater under way. The arts center over here is operated by the City. We think

that's very important to our City. And that brings industry in too because people in industry like to feel that everything is there for them. They like Boston and the big cities because they have all the concerts and theater. We need that here in order to assure people.

Development and Ideologies of Economic Growth

The subfield of economic development was created after the Second World War. Changes in the structure of the world economic system and the decolonization of Third World countries resulted in new relationships between industries and state systems, fostering new strategies and new ideologies for capitalist expansion.

The dominant ideology of the 1950s and 1960s, in which all economies were thought to "travel along a linear path" (in Rostow's [1960] terms), has been replaced with theories of neocolonialism and interdependence in the literature if not the public policy statements of dependent economies. The assumption behind Rostow's "stages" was the "trickle-down" effect created by successful capitalist accumulation and concentration, with states playing the role of redistributors to the poorer members of the economic relationship. "Dependencia" theorists also depended on the assumption of corrective action in the redistribute relationship, aptly expressed by Tanzanian President Nyerere's address to the Royal Commonwealth Society in November 1985:

> In one world, as in one state, when I am rich because you are poor, and I am poor because you are rich, the transfer of wealth from the rich to the poor is a matter of right: it is not an appropriate matter for charity. . . . If the rich nations go on getting richer and richer at the expense of the poor, the poor of the world must demand a change, in the same way as the proletariat demanded change in the past. And we do demand change. As far as we are concerned, the only question at issue is whether the change comes by dialogue or confrontation. (Quoted in Streeten, 1981:106)

The lack of success by many exploited economies to change the nature of their economic relationships is rooted in the power politics of redistribution. Because much of the development ideology, fostered by modernization or dependency theory and championed by officials, assumes that those with the highest concentrations of capital will redistribute wealth for human services including job promotion, the "confrontation" threatened by Nyerere's statement rarely takes place at the level of the state.

The ideology used by economically dominant forces, including multinational corporations, promotes the ideals of redistribution and human equality. Warner (1953) in his analysis of Memorial Day, described how rituals of collective unity could be used to manipulate levels of class inequality. Dominant classes under capitalism, particularly through advertising (Ewen, 1978), emphasize access to resources through ability and determination rather than class-based control.

Godfrey (1987) argues against the strict separation of the First and Third Worlds as many regional economies in "core" countries begin to resemble "peripheral" economies. Cardoso's (1974) "dependent-associated" development is seen in areas such as Pittsfield just as easily as it is applied to traditionally dependent national governments. While the hegemonic terminology provided by modernization theory was largely rejected by Third World nations in the 1970s, its legacy remains in regional areas being transformed by changes in the world economy and the multinationals that direct those trends. Pittsfield's lack of success in redeveloping its industry is referred to by business leaders as a problem of psychological dimensions.

The development officers we interviewed between 1982 and 1988 stressed the discontinuity between business and the community. During our first interview with the director of the Chamber of Commerce—an MBA who worked for the New York Bankers Association before moving to Pittsfield—he summed up the area's problems: "People in the Berkshires are individualistic; they are very independent. They are set in their ways about their basic concerns. Anything that brings about change they fear and resist."

This commissioner saw his job as pulling the various aspects of the community together in the development process, describing himself as "a pimp getting people together in the right direction." He voiced concern about the long-term residents of the community, who he felt were overly optimistic about the ability of General Electric to sustain an economic base for the city, and about the second home owners and tourists, who resisted change out of the fear that the natural beauty of the area would be destroyed:

> In this area there are alot of people with money, and they put their money where their mouth is, in resisting change. The Pittsfield population is 262nd in the country, while it is 62nd in medium income. Pittsfield is not like a normal tourist area, it is an elite tourist area, with education and with money. . . . What sets this community aside are neighborhood groups all over the area, representing a minority, but vocal enough to prevent development from happening.[2]

Complicating the issues of consensus about development is the leadership vacuum. The commissioner complained that part of the problem was the two-year term of the mayor, which meant that he or she was continually running for office, and the low pay that rendered the office symbolically illegitimate. Business leaders, he complained, were not providing the leadership they could: "There are business leaders in this community who would have unbelievable power, should they choose to exercise it."

The belief that the various sectors of the community are too mired in self-interest to promote development is echoed by many of those in management positions. As the director of community relations at General Electric lamented, there are two general themes that create impediments to development:

> We are surrounded by mountains, and there is a general influx of two thrusts: First, GE brings people in and takes them out—executives, like me who don't mind. I make the community wherever I am sent. Second, New Yorkers, those who come and stay and really think that this is beautiful, let's start up a restaurant, but quick, close the door behind us as we don't want this to be spoiled. West Stockbridge wants West Stockbridge the way it is. It [Pittsfield] was an isolated community for a long time; solely built in this century in pioneering work by GE. The work of transforming and GE—the community hasn't ebbed and flowed with the rest of the world.

Native versus Nonnative Views of Development

Differences between native and nonnative views are tied to differences in outlook and experience. Like the corporation, which has its management outside the area, those who ran development programs were all from other places or were brought in from outside. Long-term residents are concerned about stability and the continued functioning of the community's infrastructure. Many General Electric workers and others with a history of living with the corporation are wary of private industry interests, espousing a belief, Mayor Smith complained, "that private enterprise should be separate from government as church from state." The struggle to preserve tradition among changing circumstance produces run-ins with the nonnative views that see opportunities for capital accumulation in national trends. Development specialists, whether developers or city managers, often fail to reconcile the values of the community with the goals they seek.

The belief that General Electric built the community is at the root of the differences between native and nonnative points of view. Since 1904, General Electric prevented other companies from settling in the area, had considerable influence over the city council, employed from the same families for generations, and provided a sense of security for its employees. When the umbrella of the corporation started to break down during the 1970s, Pittsfield became analogous to a small colonial state that had just been granted independence: it had no mechanisms in place to deal with its new status.

For the generations of residents who live in Pittsfield, General Electric was an industry that was supported by the community and that was built on the community's labor. The difference in perspective generated a "we" and "they" dichotomy appearing most vividly in the deliberations of city government. This "we" and "they" is not based so much on class in Pittsfield as it is a reflection of a battle over turf and the perceived responsibility of industry to the community by management and labor. The de facto leadership—those in political or appointed office who are responsible for the maintenance of community organization—are torn between pro- and antidevelopment forces. The residents of Pittsfield reacted to the unsettling of the industrial scene in contradictory ways—relying on the corporation for guidance while aware that it was not providing continuing leadership.

The first economic development officer we interviewed (Pittsfield's first commissioner of economic development) described Pittsfield as "a community of fifty thousand run like a Ma and Pa grocery store." Born in Pittsfield but raised in and newly transplanted from Boston, she was openly frustrated by her inability to convince government officials of the necessity for a commitment to development efforts. The problem of attracting industry was exacerbated by a feeling of many that the city was not committed to the effort, leading one *Berkshire Eagle* reporter to note that "persuading the head of a growing company to locate a plant and high-paying jobs here is similar, in one respect, to training a mule: first, you have to get his attention. That can be difficult when other cities from Quincy to Haverhill are performing their own serenades" (Katz, *Berkshire Eagle*, September 15, 1980). Charlie Smith, then mayor of the city, believed that "Pittsfield's like a bubble about to burst," and was elected largely on his efforts in opposition to the Pyramid Mall, a proposed 600,000 square foot retail center. His successful opposition was backed by the community but branded the mayor antibusiness, a label that stuck throughout his term in office despite his increasing cooperation with the Chamber of Commerce. The belief that local residents are primarily antidevelopment is voiced by those involved in development efforts who have lived outside of the community. Disappointed by community in-fighting and unsuccessful attempts at industrial rezoning, this commissioner resigned from her job to become a development consultant and finally left the region entirely to work in Washington. Mayor Smith commented upon her departure that "I've always known [she] was far too talented to remain for very long in the community development position," particularly "at the salary it pays." Her replacement was recruited from city

management, a contract manager who supervised the demolition program
that leveled a large section of the west side of town. We asked him about his
relationship with the city:

> *What were you doing before you came here?*
> I was a contract manager for the city. And before that I ran a
> demolition program. . . . The outlook now seems to be more of
> rehabilitation.
> *Could you comment on that?*
> Well, you have to consider it in general terms. You have to
> relate it to the national economy. . . . Basically what we've done is
> clean up a lot of the undesirable buildings over on the west side.
> That is basically what community development is about. We
> found that there were a number of buildings that made a dent in
> the city of Pittsfield. They've been condemned for years now.
> With one man the city had been chasing this man for 20 years just
> to get this building torn down. And finally, the city had no pro-
> gram for doing this, and finally we put together this program that
> said if you cooperate with the city of Pittsfield, we'll tear down the
> building and you will hold title to the land. If you don't want to
> cooperate, we'll take you to court, and finally we'll demolish your
> house and we'll put a lien on your property. Using that approach
> about two and a half years ago we started this demolition process.
> We've taken about 50 houses today, over on Dewey and Robinson
> and places like that. . . . After tearing those houses down, in a very
> short period of time, it's turned those neighborhoods around. All
> of a sudden you have a vacant lot that is seeded over and they are
> taking pride in their houses, they've put fences up and they've
> started mowing their lawns. They have a real pride in the neigh-
> borhood because these real eyesores are gone. They don't have to
> live with it any more in their lives.

Cosmetic changes to Pittsfield's neglected houses reflected an attempt
by city managers to generate enthusiasm among community residents who
were becoming dissatisfied with city management, and who were convinced
that the economic scene was deteriorating. Faced with the problem of a
small city government trying to bring redevelopment to an area long supervised by General Electric, the mayor appointed the Fisher Group from Troy,
New York, as the developer for the large downtown parcel. The appoint-
ment caused concern that the Housing Authority's purview was being
eroded and that outside interests were being favored. During the meeting
held to discuss the issue, the Fisher Group "urged" immediate action, and
when it was suggested that other developers be interviewed, told the assem-

bled city administrators that "to come back, we had to put four other opportunities on the shelf. . . . We have to know where we stand. If the city has any
interest in us, say 'Come on, let's go' with all alacrity and speed"[3] (*Berkshire
Eagle*, July 10, 1981).

The second commissioner of community and economic development
saw his role as one integrating industrial and community development, coop-
erating with the Chamber of Commerce's interest in attracting outside businesses while maintaining and improving the beauty of the area. The delicate
balance between the city council's mistrust of industrial development and
the need for industrial zoning could be handled, he felt, by good planning
and communication among the concerned parties. A major problem
acknowledged by all was the lack of appropriately zoned land and the resistance by many in the community to changes in zoning standards. The commissioner succeeded in rezoning 400 acres for industrial development.
When we asked him how he accomplished this, he responded:

> Well, I think it was the way it was handled and I think it was a
> question of timing, too. There was a need for it and I think that it
> was handled correctly. See we involved them in the process and
> we told them what we were going to do and why we were going
> to do it.

Despite efforts toward new industrial development, this commissioner
believed that new initiatives at General Electric would point to further development, just as many of the community's residents believed that the corporation could "recover" from its downsizing. The GE Plastics Technology
Center was seen by the commissioner (and by many others) as a catalyst for
new startups in plastics and lighting technology, a hope that had an historical
basis in the branching out by employees of GE Plastics in the 1950s to small
entreprenuerial firms. The Plastics Center only employed some fifty odd
engineers. Still, the commissioner commented,

> General Electric is bringing a lot of high-priced talent into the
> Pittsfield market and it's a transforming effect. What's happening
> here now is that Pittsfield's population itself has been transformed
> from a tank town to a high collar, very professional yuppie type. . . .
> And the whole outlook of GE and the city of Pittsfield in the support
> services, the educational system and so forth has changed. There's a
> great demand for artistic and cultural resources that we already had
> before. We have a community art center that ten years before we
> didn't. There's also a public theater in town. There's the Berkshire
> Ballet and other institutions.

The search for new development was hampered by a shrinking tax base, unsuccessful attempts to lure new manufacturing industry, and the ambivalence of the community toward development as the city's managers were defining it. Tourism, services and manufacturing development were often mentioned in interviews with city officials as on the rise despite overwhelming evidence to the contrary. In the scramble to prove that progress was being made, officials burned out in continual fights over turf. When we first visited the director of the Berkshire Economic Revitalization Corporation, we noted that his offices were in the basement of a peripherally located building where he functioned with a half-time secretary. The final demise of his organization was attributed to the city council members who voted against the continued funding of the organization because of its failure to attract industry, but it was more widely attributed to the organization's lack of political connections to factional city interests.

The second commissioner of community and economic development left in 1986 to work for the area's congressman. He did leave visible signs of development: plans for an airport connector road and a designated industrial park. The city was still unable, however, to attract substantial outside industry and had lost the only commercial airline that called the airport complex home.

I joked with the third commissioner of community and economic development that when I was told a new person had been hired to fill the post, I wondered whether the job wasn't toxic. The commissioner laughed but knowingly related his background as a city planner and administrator from a neighboring state, stating that he could "assimilate what's going on and draw some very, what I think are very valid conclusions, but I sure can't defend them in public, I sure can't prove them. The bulk of what I see happening, the public doesn't want to hear." Like his predecessors, this manager believed that industry could be attracted to Pittsfield if the conditions were right, and that the area would benefit from the state's prominence in the computer industry and General Electric's plastics division. When asked why he came to Pittsfield, he responded:

> Pittsfield is one of the few towns, few communities I looked at as having an interesting opportunity. Pittsfield is the type of community where it can balance the split between service industries and manufacturing and make a goal of it. Most communities I see now [are necessarily] making the economic transition into service industry, with manufacturing very rapidly declining. Pittsfield because of its central location among the computer firms and other related type industries, we need to clean up the issue of the bypass, get it linked to the interstate. I think you'd see Pittsfield blossom as an entirely new industrial revolution here.

So you think the bypass is the main issue here?
Without a link to the interstate I don't think that will happen
here, in any great or substantial manner. But if it does happen,
you'll see it happen so fast it will be mind boggling to the people
here.

Like his predecessors, this commissioner believed that the only hope
for development was in changes in attitude on the part of the city's residents
that would generate a "take-off" in the economy. Although he was more real-
istic about the role of the major corporation and the constraints under which
the city operated, his optimism was rooted in development strategies that
focused on individuals:

> You always have four, five, five basic issues to be balanced. You
> have tourism, industry, large-scale commercial, housing, and I
> can't remember the fifth, oh, service industries as opposed to
> manufacturing industries. You have those basic competing uses. I
> would say as recently as five years ago, most people would con-
> sider them incompatible. Nowadays communities such as Pitts-
> field are beginning to realize that they are not only not
> incompatible, they are specifically in effect compatible. That is a
> key attitudinal change in Pittsfield. Without that attitude, I would
> have a gloomy forecast for the next five years. Because that atti-
> tude has changed significantly and is still changing in a favorable
> direction, I see the growth potential there.

Uneven Development and Relations of Dependency

Uneven development, where one sector of the economy is developing or
declining more rapidly than another, is witnessed most clearly in towns and
cities where the economy is controlled by a multinational. Bluestone (1972)
commented that the "dynamics of the American economy are best described
by the law of uneven development. Those who control capital resources in
the economy will tend over time to reinvest in those particular product lines,
machinery, geographical areas, and workers which promise the highest
return on dollar investment" (1972:66). This process results in the concentration of industrial assets and wealth within a small circle of industrialists
who have a disproportionate influence in political circles. The consequence
in Pittsfield, predictably, was the lopsided influence of General Electric in all
development decisions. For multinational corporations, development is synonymous with an increase in capital accumulation. Unlike family, labor, and
community strategies, this development is unconcerned with human issues
and focused on the expansion of capital.

For many years, power transformers were a profitable industry for the General Electric corporation and thus were a successful enterprise in the community. Even at the time the power transformer division was closed in Pittsfield, it was still profitable. When the division failed to keep up with the pace of capital accumulation in the corporation's other divisions, it was shut down. The human interface between this decision and the effects on the community were not important enough to forestall the redirection of capital into more profitable concerns.

Outside of industrial development, however, the community has been the lesser player in development processes as well. Pittsfield watched the tremendous growth in summer arts tourism—music, theater, and dance—for years as tourists flocked to Jacob's Pillow, Tanglewood, the Williamstown Theater Festival, and other cultural institutions. The community tried to capitalize on this interest with the formation of the Berkshire Ballet and the Berkshire Public Theater, and the city entered the ring with ARTABOUT, a short-lived arts festival in the early 1980s. As with industrial development, the city was a secondary player in the tourist development around it. Like industrial developers, tourists tend to invest their time and capital into known quantities with a history and a track record. While the Berkshire Ballet and the Public Theater survived, they did not begin to approach the successful operation of their more mature cousins. ARTABOUT was discontinued after failing to attract significant attention.

As the community attempted to find workable redevelopment strategies, the reality of uneven development continually reappears in the form of reputation (companies wary of competing for labor with a multinational, for example, are hesitant to move in), or though infrastructures. While the corporation claims to have stopped playing the role of community economic development director, its past practices and future directions, and even the physical presence of its buildings, have a major effect on the direction of redevelopment issues and strategies.

The General Electric Donation

The largest single effort at initiating an infrastructure for new industry was provided by General Electric. The city proposed an innovative idea for an "incubator facility"—a building that could be divided up into small spaces for startup companies that could share bookkeeping, a typing pool, copying facilities, and professional services such as a lawyer and an accountant. The commissioner explained that he didn't

> know all of the details, the mayor was involved with GE, and what was actually taking place in the course of the conversations was that GE was going to vacate a number of buildings, GE was also

looking at how to dispose of a number of buildings which were subject to being torn down because they weren't suitable for renovation, other buildings were considered feasible but weren't determined yet as to what their usefulness was. And of course over in Schenectady they had just done the thing with donating the building. I think that is what actually occurred or they were in the course of looking at it. But there was an idea that there was something that might work in Pittsfield as well.

Enthusiasm was tempered from the start by GE's condition that the building be accepted by the city sight unseen. Pittsfield was in the middle of a major conflict brought about by retired GE workers concerned with PCB residues left from transformer production, and was concerned about entering into agreements that might make the city liable for cleanup efforts. Although there was general optimism about the donation, the commissioner agreed with other city administrators that it had to be conditional:

> *Did they know which building it was?*
> We have some idea of which building it might have been, but no confirmation from GE. . . . I was one of the parties that made a very strong recommendation that if the building were offered, that the city's acceptance of it be contingent on a 90 day period in which environmental testing and several other works would be done in checking the feasibility of reuse of the building. If that were in fact found to be such that everything were found to be okay, there were no problems, maintenance of the building made sense, there were no environmental issues involved with it, all of the various things that might be potential problems if we moved an industry into it, everything came out perfectly fine, then we ought to be looking at accepting the building.

The city's reluctance came as a shock to the corporation, which was counting on the donation as good public relations and a substantial tax write-off. It was clear that the tax aspect was, in the commissioner's words, a "dead givaway." Unused to the city government's assertiveness, a scramble ensued:

> There were a series of management type analyses that were done by GE. We had input into them in some respects, but mostly it was an internal matter. And there was a waiting period, I think it was mid-December before we were notified that GE for its own corporate reasons had some legal issues involved. I think one of the things that was cited was security within their own plant compound. But they had some serious corporate legal issues that were involved, there were some management decisions that were not

able to be made in a timely manner. They didn't know themselves that they could safely give us a building, and therefore as it was important that it occur before the end of the calendar year they did not believe that it was possible. Then after the first of January we were simply verbally from an official source advised that the offer which was being considered was no longer open to discussion. It was a closed subject.

Although the problem of pollution was never discussed, when we interviewed the commissioner six months later, he was more open:

Building 100, as we discussed at the time has been resolved, its not available to the city or to anyone else for that matter, as is the case with a number of other buildings there which were looked at, because there was a concern that there might be the pollution problems, they were very carefully not stating that there was a pollution problem but concerned that there might be, and therefore did not want to raise the possibility of either inflicting that problem on someone else or incurring the additional liability as the case may be. . . . It's a very substantial area and they found various deposits of pollutants on an adjoining property, again a company that was in the process of a major expansion, the expansion process has been shut down for over a year now as a result of finding the pollution.

The influence of the corporation over development efforts extends beyond the city's willingness to confront the issue. While claiming that they can "no longer be Daddy Warbucks," General Electric dismissed the fears of wide spread pollution and made it clear that direct confrontations would threaten "the viability" if the corporation's ties with the city. Pressed to find more directions for development efforts, and hampered by a history of corporate control over community affairs, development planning was left to avenues that did not impinge on the corporation's territory. The city's relationship with the corporation was restructured to accept a lessened public presence, while the city was still forced to play a secondary role in long-term development efforts. The commissioner's position as an outsider involved in local administrative efforts allowed him to take a harder line on General Electric's actions at the same time that it kept him from the internal dynamics of the city's relationships with the corporation (as commissioner of community and economic development, he was kept unaware of the initial discussions about the building donation). It was perhaps the first time, however, that the corporation had been openly questioned about the responsibility for its intentions, an action that marked a change in community assertiveness.

Bypasses and Parking Lots

Capital mobility in late capitalism has produced a culture that runs. Corporations and companies run to different regions and offshore in search of cheap labor; workers run from one company to another seeking employment and stores run from one section of the city to another in search of customers. Though the mode of transportation differs, mobility is at the center of the community's relations of power. While corporations manipulate capital flight through microprocessor technology, families are dependent on their cars for movement. The development of a culture dependent on cars in the United States has been one of the most sustained reactions to capitalist development, encouraged by the car manufacturers and providing options to individuals that their pre-car counterparts were without.

Parking lots and the issue of parking have continually been debated in Pittsfield. No one argues that there is adequate parking—the conflicts stem from how parking garages are to be financed and how much tourists and residents will be forced to pay for the privilege. Federal money first became available for a parking garage downtown in the early 1980s when it was assumed that the Pyramid Companies would build a retail mall downtown. The plans for the garage were rejected with that of the mall and a new opportunity did not arise until 1985. Hit with declining sales in downtown stores, and the movement of stores from the city's main street to the new mall outside of the city, one city councilman suggested that the answer was in providing diagonal parking instead of the traditional parallel mode. Parking was seen as a sign of deterioration or progress as negotiations around more substantial efforts stalled. That the opening of the new parking garage in 1988 was also late in opening prompted the *Berkshire Eagle* to declare "Pittsfield: Where Bulldozers Just Doze":

> The announcement last week that the new $8 million downtown parking garage wouldn't open on time had a sadly familiar ring to it. . . . So it goes with at least half a dozen other major public works projects in Pittsfield: They seem to take years to materialize, if they happen at all. To newcomer and native alike, this city seems a place where ideas linger for decades, opportunities come and go and nothing happens fast.

> The development of the urban renewal property behind North Street, vacant since the 1960s, is a good illustration of the phenomenon. After the Pyramid Companies, the developers of the Berkshire Mall in Lanesboro, abandoned their plans for a suburban-style shopping mall there in 1980, the city struggled for years to lure other types of development. It ended up building the

parking garage as an enticement for office-building growth. Now even that will be late. (*Berkshire Eagle*, March 20, 1988).

The need to quickly generate cash revenues in a declining economy generates symbols that encapsulate condensed versions of a community in trouble. It is not surprising that in a culture transformed by the automobile industry, the issue of a bypass to provide access to the Massachusetts Turnpike has been a point of contention since the late 1940s.[4] Waves of support and opposition by community groups and political parties came and went depending on the political atmosphere and the trends in vogue among GE and city managers. Proponents of the bypass argued that improved transportation in and around Pittsfield would encourage industry to expand and would attract outside industries. Those opposed worried that a bypass for truck and other through traffic around Pittsfield would hurt the character of the Berkshires and encourage shopping centers around the highway rather than the downtown sector.

The bypass issue abated until 1981, when the city decided to hold a referendum. The vote passed in favor of a bypass road, only to be thwarted by the lack of funding to build it. Throughout the decade of the 1980s, discussions and debates continued on the federal, state, and local levels concerning the financing of the road. Governor Dukakis campaigned in 1982 in support of the bypass and his election paved the way for state approval if funds could be found. By 1988, when it looked like funds could be allocated, another referendum was held. Unlike the first, this polling resulted in an upset victory for the bypass's opponents, who vowed to remain active. As one told us, "you can have a referendum, but the state just seems to keep on rolling. They have time on their side, and they have method on their side. They wear people down."

The referendum was not binding and although the new mayor campaigned against it during her election, the first stages of the road were being built by the late fall of 1988.

The bypass, like the problem with parking, embodies the contradictions of city government. There is an awareness that city government must be responsive to the community at the same time that it appeases the wishes of industry. Mayor Smith was clear in his assessment of the importance of the working population when he told us in 1984 that

> First of all, no one gets elected unless the blue collar worker is behind him. No one gets elected. I don't care whether it's here, or at the state level, or the president of the United States. If you don't have the working-class people with you, you are not going to get elected to public office. The difficulty comes in when a major or a governor, or any elected official begins to work with Big Business.

If you're not careful, you can be tagged as Big Business oriented and that you're not taking care of the working man. You have to be able to relate to working-class people, that everything that you're doing helping business and industry, and the large corporations, is there to ensure them that they have jobs and that their children have jobs and that everything is directly for the working class.

Obliged to respond to both private and public sector interests, city managers were forced to compromise and defend their opinions. Although the mayor and his staff operated within the framework that business provided them, the attempts at consensus that reelection requires often frustrates efforts. The creation of chaos requires that social scientists studying the restructuring of communities go beyond traditional analyses. The day-to-day working relationships of the community run against the "reasoning" proposed by academic planning experts (Friedman, 1987). The inability to carry out planning efforts, or to plan at all, has itself become a major issue in Pittsfield. The mayor elected in 1988 won on a platform that vowed "to restore 'vision' and long-range planning to city government."

Mall Wars

Like the bypass, debates over the existence and placement of a major retail mall plagued the community for nearly twenty years. The height of the conflict occurred in 1981, when a plan for a downtown mall proposed by the Pyramid Companies was rejected by the mayor. The Pyramid Companies sued the city, claiming that it had an understanding with the previous administration for the project. The friction between the mayor and the mall developers became another symbol of the differences between the private and the public sector, between businesses represented by the Chamber of Commerce and local government.

Local residents were worried about the effect of the mall on the downtown area, an already declining section of the city. The wish to keep the original street plans intact prompted city officials to build a model of Pittsfield as it looked at the beginning of the century. The development commissioner told us:

The reason we did that is that we wanted to show people what it looked like and how it evolved. In fact, the downtown has its own character and spirit. The idea is that the downtown will respond when the market is there. The Pyramid project was an ambitious project—what would have happened there is that it would have dwarfed everything around it. . . . [I]t would have annihilated all of North Street, and there would have been vacant stores all up and down North Street. They might have busted and we would have had North street on our hands. But basically North Street twenty five years ago, North and West Streets were complementary to each other, like two limbs of a body. . . . In addition to having a number of stores and shops down on West Street, there were three major restaurants and a train station in a half-mile. It was a very, very beautiful quintessential New England type of town. That was destroyed in the old 1967 urban type of philosophy. And they took down a lot of houses around there. They destroyed them—you can see the houses up on the hill. That was basically the economic base for downtown Pittsfield. They did their business downtown. They wiped them out of there and they wiped out a lot of the stores and you are operating basically on one lung. Now it's coming back to a philosophy we think is appropriate to downtown Pittsfield. Shopping centers are certainly appropriate, there are plenty of them to go around. But Pittsfield is different. The per capital income of Pittsfield is about $18,000. We're also in terms of surveys one of the highest communities for per capita savings. So there's a great market here for a good quality store. It's going to happen and I think we've been on a ten-year decline primarily to the GE. But the decline has slowed up to nothing now and is practically at a breakeven.

The Pyramid Companies lost their suit and the mayor was eventually able to convince the Chamber (at least publicly), that it was his intention to work with them. The end of the lawsuit, however, was not the end of the mall story. What ensued was a seven-year free-for-all where other developers saw opportunities open up and the city became increasingly involved in conflicts over the direction of development and the need for tax revenues. Pyramid Companies relocated the site of their mall outside of the city limits and commenced building without permits. Two other developers, Melvin-Simon Associates and ShopCo, proposed plans for malls, but their permits deadlocked in the city council. The commissioner's analysis of the situation in 1987 was that

> Pyramid is going to get built, unless ShopCo or Coltsville does. Pyramid already started construction without legal permits. That's stopped, but they'll be back in business before too long, given the chance. Pittsfield holds one vital card on Pyramid. They need a sewer connection. They have to come to Pittsfield. So far they've been told what they can do with their sewer connection. Put it to

use early. Shopco has been denied its curbcuts. No curbcuts, no stores. That leaves Shopco remaining. The city, for fiscal reasons has a desperate need to assure that the shopping mall ends up within city lines, Pittsfield, any one of the three, Pittsfield is going to have all the impact, negative fiscal impacts. No matter how you slice it, Pittsfield will get virtually 100 percent. There'll be some spillover, maybe Lanesboro, other towns in general, but the severest impacts will be on Pittsfield. Pittsfield already has been headed for fiscal problems, without or with any mall being built. . . . The City has a need to see an additional set of values that range from 30 to 50 million dollars.

As the Pyramid Companies started building, the stores on North Street in downtown Pittsfield began making plans to relocate. The largest department store closed its doors in 1987, citing financial difficulties. The fight between the Pyramid Companies and the city continued as permits were denied and environmental impact statements enforced. Pyramid had constructed the shell for the mall on wetlands purchased from a local family in the most expensive land deal in Berkshire County history. The land was bought for $12,368,743 or $108,498 an acre. The *Berkshire Eagle* and other local papers, as well as the *New York Times*, followed the progress of the fight between outside developer and city, prompting daily stories that took on a ring of soap opera discourse. In its news analysis of the mall war, the *Berkshire Eagle* (March 20, 1988) noted that the Pyramid Companies of Syracuse had a history of building without permission and overriding local concerns: "For years, the Pyramid Companies of Syracuse have quietly altered the physical and political landscape of New York and New England, building huge upscale shopping malls and shaping the local governments that permitted them." The company regularly chooses "environmentally sensitive properties" and then "hired ex-governors, environmental agency lawyers, a town judge and a local legislative leader to plead its construction cause" (ibid.). The company was under investigation in three states, and was accused of buying elections by the New York Commission on Government Integrity. As *The Eagle* reported, "The commission last year uncovered evidence that Pyramid and the New York Republican State Committee joined forces to finance a 1985 town council race in Poughkeepsie at the time Pyramid needed a pro-mall council to approve plans for its 1 million square foot Galleria there" (ibid.).

The dispute over the Pyramid Companies operation gave local officials fuel for their position, and in 1988 the mall stood finished but idle. Unable to open because of disputes over water rights, the mall was having major difficulties attracting workers at the offered wages. The mall finally succeeded in obtaining water rights by offering a $2 million "hook-up" charge, the first installment delivered after the new mayor secretly provided water. The move was hotly contested in the city council, and reminiscent of the tactics GE used to obtain approval of its own plans in the past, one councilor accused the new mayor of incompetence and selling out to powerful developers: "What this means is that Pyramid is in control of the city. . . . It shows how they corrupt the governmental process. . . . They created an invisible, secret government to achieve what they could not achieve above board."

The other two developers were still eyeing construction in Pittsfield despite the fact that the Pyramid Companies could not attract the upscale tenants they had envisioned. The upturn in tourism in the area continues to attract retail hopes as the fears for the downtown area have become realized.

Ideology and Community Crisis

Ideology has a major function in the maintenance of social order in class-based societies. Marx asserted in *The German Ideology* that the ruling class is expressed by ruling ideas, "ideas which become the ruling ideas of an epoch" (Ricoeur, 1986:254). Besides the simple expression of dominance, however, ideology has three important functions. As Ricoeur (1986) summarizes, ideology serves as systematic distortion, as a mode of the legitimating of power and as a mode of integration. The schemata of ideology as an integrating principal Ricoeur borrows from Geertz, who tells us that "it is through the construction of ideologies, schematic images of social order, that man makes himself for better or worse a political animal" (quoted in Ricoeur, 1986:218).

Pittsfield was a community in crisis. The genesis of the crisis is international as well as local; it reflects a basic restructuring of the capitalist system on a world scale. The means by which Pittsfield's population has adapted to changes in the economic scene are contradictory, with acts of compliance and resistance. Hoping that the economic status quo—the corporation—will support the community as it has in the past, there was no active signs of struggle against the company. The "negotiated class struggle" was still taking place in the context of union and management, although little real negotiation takes place when entire divisions of production are closed down. What is more complex is the economic negotiation by which the community functions as a corporate entity. Worldwide restructuring has forced community management to confront issues of employment and tax revenues. The context of the battle, however, is in the realm of ideology. Ideology in Pittsfield serves as distortion as it positions the corporation in a place without alternatives, "responding to the market," or "keeping the corporation economically viable." The corporation is presented as an entity simply doing what it has to do. It functions as legitimation as in Ricoeur's terms, "a claim to authority made by all forms of authority." City managers and development specialists, whether they be public or privately oriented, struggle to have their positions validated.

Reactions that are not in keeping with stated goals are by necessity rejected and labeled as counterproductive. The insistence by business and outside investors that "attitudes need to be changed" is a direct attack on opinions that run counter to stated development strategies. The ultimate goal is the provision of an atmosphere conducive to the attraction of private industry and the investment of capital.

The resistance expressed by homeowners, workers, and families to the development process is not a clear indication of class struggle but an adaptive strategy for the maintenance of community. Workers accept or reject the wishes of their employers according to material conditions (Brook and Finn, 1986:125). Pittsfield's population fits into Stearns's description of working-class culture as "a preservation of tradition amid admittedly changing circumstances" (1980:626). The material conditions of restructuring in Pittsfield are lowering the standard of living. Even while unemployment is increasing, service sector industries are finding it difficult to recruit the workers they require. Workers who have been laid off from the General Electric plant and others unable to find jobs left the area rather than accept employment beneath the standard the area has enjoyed. The new retail mall found it so difficult to staff its establishments that it has asked the federal government for permission to recruit labor from Mexico and Latin America.

The development strategies proposed were not successful and the ambivalence and resistance on the part of the population frustrated capital investors. More significantly, union members have refused to accept lower standards for companies being wooed by the city than those that they won in years of struggle. One relatively large company, for example, had planned to move to Pittsfield but ultimately decided against it after statements made by a local union leader and the mayor regarding their labor practices. The commissioner of economic development told the story in 1987:

> We just tried, we just lost a large firm, looking for 128,000 square feet. We had everything put together, they took a union vote, the union voted it down, head of one of the local labor unions and the mayor both made some statements, caused the company great upset. They were all set to lay it to rest, to sign the dotted line to move here. The combination of the two statements in quick succession led the company to say wait a minute, let's rethink this.

The labor union leader at GE commented that

There was absolutely no question that in their opinion that industry was trying to bale out of a union situation and when they hit
the ground in Pittsfield they're going to be unionized and it's
going to be a tough stand. That scared the hell out of the company.
And the mayor's comment was to the effect that the company had
used Pittsfield, had not dealt with us in good faith, had used us.

They were looking at confronting a union issue, not a tough
stand. What the union did was instead of essentially serving notice
that we do anticipate unionizing you, but being reasonable about
how we do it, they took the position that we're going to union
you, we're going to be very tough about it, you're going to pay a
price for having screwed the union down in Waterbury.

Lack of consensus on the development process and the pull of city government between public and private concerns led to attempts at "quick
fixes" such as the parking garage. The first priority is the generation of tax
revenues that can sustain the infrastructure of the community. Another
development attempt concentrated on the small industries that already
existed in the community, and that sustained growth during a period of
major decline. This was the small plastics industry, started by small entrepreneurs whose success caused Pittsfield to be recognized as "the Plastics
Capital of America."

CHAPTER 7

Uneven Development and Community Response

The restructuring of industry in Pittsfield presents challenges to residents try-ing to maintain continuity. Responses to economic change encompassed all of the features of kinship, friendship, and trust available to counter the increased alienation that realingnment presents.

The legacy of modernization theory has led to a renewed interest in the place of entrepreneurs in development strategies. Unlike the proponents of modernization theory, who focus on individual actors in the marketplace, more recent theories of entrepreneurial activity analyze the social relation-ships in the context of the "opportunity structure" (defined as the economic, social, technological, and political conditions) that exist in any given histori-cal period (Greenfield, Stricken, and Aubrey, 1979). Benedict (1968) shows how families are factored into the development process as claims to kin-based loyalty work to the advantage of new enterprises. In Pittsfield, kinship and friendship have figured largely in entrepreneurial activity.

The major portion of sustained entrepreneurial activity in Pittsfield occurred as a direct reaction to corporate decisions at General Electric. The entrepreneurial activity attempted to maintain families while furthering eco-nomic and community goals and led to a growing industrial base.

Plastics Firms and Uneven Development

The operative word in Pittsfield, particularly during the early 1980s, was plastics. It still is. Reminiscent of the industrialist's advice to the college stu-dent in *The Graduate*, plastics operations were the wave of the future. Many of the new plastics firms occupied abandoned mill sites, symbolically affirm-

77

ing their ties to the community. While, in appearance, the development of the small firms parallels that of its predecessors a century or more before, the differences are striking.

In 1987, there were twenty-six plastics firms in the Pittsfield area employing 1,200 people, roughly the same number that worked for the GE plastics division in the late 1940s. By 1997, there were thirty-eight firms, employing approximately 1,800 individuals, or 3.5 percent of total private employment. These firms are outgrowths of the GE plastics moldmaking division that ceased production in 1953 and that saw the last vestiges of its plastics operation, Genal, dismantled in 1983. The plastics firms in Pittsfield were viewed by optimistic residents as the Berkshire's answer to Route 128 around Boston or to California's Silicon Valley. They represented an independent proliferation of industry not financially dependent on the past source of industrial development, General Electric. Development planners claimed that the corporation's "commitment" by way of placing its international plastics research and development headquarters in Pittsfield would encourage industrial plastics growth, although it is equally obvious that these two industrial complexes had very different resources, and operated in very distinct contextual bases.

The first industrial plastics moldmaking plant, Moldmasters, was established in 1946 by Tom Kushi in a shop near a grocery store in the Lakewood area of Pittsfield. Kushi had worked in the GE plant and the local high school. His first customer was the Sprague Electric plant in North Adams. He benefited from his association with General Electric managers, who sent work his way. Soon after Moldmasters was established, a group of toolmakers from General Electric's chemical division (as the plastics division was then known) left to establish Marland Mold, a larger firm that spawned the majority of subsequent development.

By 1984, there were sixteen independent moldmaking companies tracing their roots directly to General Electric (*Berkshire Eagle Review*, January 28, 1984). One mold operator told us:

> In the 1940s, General Electric plastics included 100 employees making molds. When they closed down production, some of the men who had been trained in GE plastics opened up their own shops: Marland Mold, Modern Mold, Moldmaster Engineers. Others evolved into moldmaking in the late 1940s as a result of the spurt in local companies with the departure of GE. I was at GE and left in 1953.

There were ten firms in the Berkshires using the molds made by the moldmaking operations to make plastic products. These companies also traced their evolution from the General Electric plant and the training that the founders received there. Unlike the mold-producing companies, however, these firms were likely to be allied with large conglomerates who purchased the large quantities of "widgets" (by blowing, injecting, or stamping plastic materials into mold cavities) that became the property of the purchasers.

Kinship, Friendship, and the Entrepreneurial Spirit

The role of kinship and friendship in the small firms in Pittsfield is recognized by the participants who built the industries, just as it is recognized that a common workplace generated the skill and knowledge that underpinned the new industries.

The backgrounds of the moldmaking and the plastic injection firms are traced through General Electric and to the Lakewood community, where many Italian workers found their homes before, during, and immediately after the Second World War. When we asked one of its residents and a former mayor of Pittsfield what it was like to live there, he responded that

> In the Lakewood area, most of the people work for the General Electric. . . . It is an older area, many of the homes are old, but they are very well kept. Lakewood has always been a community, like the North End of Boston. We have some problems but everyone knows who they are. You don't even have to say anything; it's just—"watch that fellow" and that takes care of it. Back ago, you didn't have police coming down here; they wouldn't come down here. We had our own police. Everyone knew what was going on.

An atmosphere of obligation and trust existed in the community, paralleling Stricken's findings among entrepreneurs in rural Wisconsin. Stricken writes that there was a

> relationship with their own people based upon "trust," a concept which they themselves articulated and which remains within the contemporary community as an understanding necessary for business activity. . . . [C]rucial to this concept of trust is the related concept of honoring one's word, of meeting one's obligations and responsibilities, without the need to force compliance. This is not to say that no sanctions are involved. Rather, failure to fulfill one's obligations is met first with internal sanctions, the rupture of social relations, and the loss of reputation in the wider community which will sharply strain relations in the future. To go beyond informal sanctions and to appeal to impersonal agencies repre-

sents a total breakdown in a relationship based on trust. (1979:160)

There was a Plastics Alumni Association (now overshadowed by the Berkshire Plastics Network) that represented past and present workers from Marland Mold and the Chemical Division at the plant. The firms have bowling teams that compete on Friday nights, throw summer clambakes, and are active in industry-specific self-help alliances that monitor markets and available technology. These ties are reinforced by the friendship and kinship ties that extend over generations. Kinship served as the basis for new industry as sons, brothers, and in-laws are trained and branch out into their own businesses. Members of the Rufo family, for example, which started Lakewood Mold after George Rufo's apprenticeship at Marland, opened the injection firms of Polymatrix and Syntronics, securing a market to which the parent firm could distribute its products.

The office where we met Bill Rufo at Polymatrix was large, carpeted, and filled with the heads of the moose he bagged during hunting season. The size and furnishings of offices at the plastics firms were directly related to the age of the firms and the position of the owners in their extended families. This office offered music as white noise to complement the wood paneling, giving the office a denlike quality. George grew up in Pittsfield, although not in the Lakewood section. His first job was with a brother who owned an auto body business. He then worked at the GE plant in distribution transformers for thirteen years, before leaving to join another brother's company, Lakewood Mold, located across the street. He was the sole owner of Polymatrix, started with three partners in 1975. The business began with five women assemblers and three men who functioned as the molding managers. The plant, in 1987, had a shifting population of eighty-five employees, the majority of them women who assembled the cassette boxes that supplied one-quarter of the U.S. market for audiotape housings. The seven men are the shift managers and mold engineers. The company initially had customers in Maine, and as Bill told us, "Our market exposure in tooling gave us a sense of its future. We actually underestimated the demand." At the time of our interview, the firm was in the process of expansion with funds from the Massachusetts Industrial Finance Association, tax bonds that have no restrictions on their use. Polymatrix, like most of the small plastics firms in the area, had never asked for nor received funds from the city of Pittsfield or other Massachusetts agencies established for development purposes.

The diversification of Lakewood Mold into plastic injection businesses preserved kinship ties by offering opportunities to siblings and offspring. It was an incentive for family members to stay in Pittsfield when they might have been forced to leave in search of employment. Asked what he considered to be Pittsfield's advantages, George Rufo Jr., the son of the founder, laughed. He explained to us that his business did not depend on the local economy: their market stretched from Massachusetts to California and they did not use General Electric products. Furthermore, he stated that the existing infrastructure of the town worked against attracting industry and was a disadvantage for the industry located there:

> Taxes are on the high side, and there is no incentive for the companies to locate in Pittsfield. There is no stimulus for business in general. The area is kind of depressed. If you get on a plane and travel for an hour in any direction, you see industry developing and happening, while that doesn't seem to be going on around here. The road system in Pittsfield is less than desirable, there is still no bypass, which they have been talking about for the past thirty years. The water system here is marginal; the sewer system is overtaxed—you need facilities to attract people.

Relationships of trust bound families together, excluding those from the outside. Most of the people who work at the small plants were raised in Pittsfield. There is a code of secrecy regarding current and potential clients, employment, and the technology used to make the products. Information is not freely offered to nonkinship allied firms or to outsiders. We found that it was easier to obtain information from newer businesses trying to establish themselves. The code of secrecy is heightened by the competition for customers and the fear of union organization.

There was a myth generated by development personnel that the firms relied on GE for business. The opposite was mostly the case. Firm owners, moldmakers and injection molders alike, combed the country for potential sales and dealt competitively with their geographic neighbors. Lakewood Mold, for example, did some limited work for General Electric, but survived largely on its relationship with companies such as IBM, Memorex, Bell and Howell, RCA, Proctor and Gamble, and Westinghouse. For its part, General Electric more often contracted outside the community for the testing and production of plastic products rather than relying on the sources at hand.

The entrepreneurial spirit comes from a sense that is supported by generations of work skills learned in the General Electric plant. Nearly all of the owners cited knowledge of the work process, products, and potential markets either through personal experience or that of family members as the basis for starting their own firms.

It is a side of the class struggle that is not often recognized: the gaining of experience in the workplace and knowledge of the work process that lessens the alienation of labor. George Rufo pointed to his father, who worked at GE ordnance, as his inspiring guide, while others saw the profit to be made while working at the General Electric plant and noted the marketing techniques that their division employed. The support of kin and friendship groups works against Nash's fourth source of alienation, that of the worker from the community.

We talked with the owner of one of the newest firms, who grew up in Pittsfield and was part of the extended kinship network that makes up the community. Richard Rilla worked for George Rufo Sr. at Marland Mold. Part of the "second generation" of firm entrepreneurs who were at Marland (along with Pyramid Mold Inc. and DAP Tool in Biddeford, Maine) we asked him to tell us how he came to start his business:

> My experience began first of all in the local high school, in the vocational education department, taking the machine shop course in the early fifties, graduated out of there in 1956, and took an apprenticeship at Marland Mold College, which was then located on Newell Street. . . . My experience grew with them and two other companies. I went to Lakewood Mold as a supervisor, and there I saw a need, or a recognition of my own personal worth and decided to start my own company. I had an opportunity four years ago to buy American Mold and Tools out. At that point he was just a one-man operation and he just wanted to retire. I bought all of his equipment, fixtures, and mold tools. With that came an immediate purchase order work, an existing customer that was located in New Jersey. Now I have seven full-time employees and three part-time employees. . . . One woman who happens to be my wife, she does part-time secretarial work, keeping the books, doing the taxes.
>
> *Are any of the people you employ your relatives or your neighbors?*
>
> Some neighbors, they happen to live in the area that I live, down in Lakewood off Newell Street. It was handy for me when I started to work. I could walk to work in the morning, and being a sixteen-year-old kid, that was very easy to do.
>
> *How much of your business is local and how much of it is out of town?*
>
> Out of town business comprises about 85–90 percent. The local GE plastics operation does have a need for moldmakers or toolmakers. Through experimental or test work they are totally involved with all the time, developing different tensile strengths for their materials, which they need to have molded and tested. They primarily go out of the area to get this work done. I know quite a few people, personal friends and relatives that work in GE plastics, and they say that there's no way that they can get the

local manufacturers to do that work because they've got people that just constantly go outside. For whatever ideological reasons they do it. They could, with what they do yearly keep five of these mold shops in Pittsfield easy, keep them totally booked.

Firm Ownership and Relations of Work

The labor-intensive character of moldmaking and injection molding presents problems in the relations of work for the employees and the owners of the firms. The relations of work in plastics are the outcome of technological deskilling. The workers are overwhelmingly women performing assembly jobs that consist of a monotonous routine with little concentration required. They work quickly in brightly lit cubicles listening to the music of their choice on headphones, acting against collaboration in the work process or the communication that might lead to unionization. National Public Radio reported in 1987 that "in 1962 we told college graduates that their future was in plastics. Now it's time to tell that to high school dropouts." The men are the skilled laborers, building the molds and managing the shops.

Beyond members of the Lakewood community, however, the men who started these firms were active in the union at General Electric. The union protected employment and entitlements and served as the basis for strengthening the community through a strong voluntary association. Yet as one owner told us,

There is no union at Polymatrix, although there was some talk about it four years ago. Ethyl is the only local plastic molding firm which has a union—they can better deal with one because they are a larger, nationally based company. They have the wherewithal to contend with unions. For a small company like Polymatrix, the union could be very harmful.

The class position of the firm owners is thus contradictory, and is analogous to Engel's description of small employers in England:

Quite as badly off under the small employers as under the manufacturers, with the single difference that they, in turn, may become small employers, and so attain a certain independence— that is to say they are at best less directly exploited by the bourgeoisie than under the factory system. Thus the small employers are neither genuine proletarians, since they live in part upon the work of their apprentices, nor genuine bourgeois, since their principal means of support is their own work. This peculiar midway position (of such small employers) . . . is to blame for their having so rarely joined wholly and unreservedly in the . . . labor movement.

The American belief in egalitarianism and upward mobility has worked, to a certain extent, for these small shop owners who are less alienated in the workplace if not more so at home. Eighty to one hundred hour weeks were normal working hours, and firm owners do not have the time to enjoy the rewards of their labor. The owners were aware of the tension between their present and past positions. Justifying the adoption of nonunion stands because of the size of their plants and the family nature of their operations, there is a sense of pride in the quality of the work produced. One of the owners of the oldest firms told us that

> We are competing with shops that hire minorities. We do our training and want workers we train since we work with expensive materials. We don't make junk. Some of the materials cost four to five dollars a pound, and our customers know what's good. They are mostly industrial concerns that are quality conscious. They check us out very carefully. We give a very thorough training.

Yet there is still a strong belief that unions should play a part in determining economic policy. The owner of a business that makes encapsulating molds told us:

> I think the unions are very negligent today in not jumping on the situation, just with this yen thing, you know, a couple of weeks ago every time you turn the TV on, they had some economist, and I don't know where these guys come from, the woodwork, but talking about the evils of the weak dollar and the strong yen, causing inflation, causing interest rates to go up, none of them talk about the fact that it could create some jobs in this country. Cheap Japanese televisions going up in price. So what, maybe we ought to make them here, you know. It's not the unions pushing on that aspect at least so the common guy could know that with those prices going up it could mean employment. I don't know, to me they are very negligent in that.

The differences between the entitlements won as union members and the owners' reaction to the "negotiated class struggle" that would provide benefits to their workers is illuminating. The problem of class relations is disguised by the competition among countries and the realities of the local economy. Referring to a bill Senator Kennedy introduced into legislation, the same owner told us:

Right now the big buzzword is competiveness, blah blah it goes on and on, they talk inherently about the currency exchange, now with the yen and wage rates abroad and what not. But you just stop and look at the mandated costs of doing business in the country. For instance, you take things for granted, we have minimum wage, today, who can survive on that anyway, but minimum wage, we have OSHA, we have the EPA, you know when I was an apprentice, I worked in places where you could have been killed, we were stepping over power lines that were just laying on the floor. I can remember a friend of mine just plugged something into an outlet and the thing exploded and he got third degree burns on his arm, and OSHA has done away with this. OSHA is good, and the EPA is good, we need minimum wage, we have to have health insurance—but, the fact of the matter is, we're being asked to compete against people who have none of these. These companies out of South Korea, and Third World nations, they're doing business like we did back at the turn of the century. I think we're cooked, right at that level, even before you get the currency exchanges stuff. To me, that is a fundamental thing, I don't see anybody addressing themselves to that. . . . And this gets back to the mandated benefits problem. To me it's a fundamental problem that is really in the beginning. Just this year they tried to push through this parenting law, which means that I think that an 18 week leave of absence, for male or female, and not only for a child, I think it involves if you have an elderly parent you got to take care of, you have to continue the benefits, and then at the end of that period they can come back and say hey, I found another job, good-bye. All of these things they keep coming out with. Kennedy is trying to push mandated benefits. The intent of all these things is great, we just cannot afford it, it's killing us.

By far the largest shop and one of the largest moldmaking concerns in the country is Ethyl Marland, which in 1983 employed 150 people. The Ethyl company of Richmond, Virginia, purchased Marland Mold and Greylock Plastics, consolidating a moldmaking and a plastics injection firm in Pittsfield in 1974, the same year that labor unrest closed one of its own plants in Puerto Rico. By purchasing the firms, Ethel guaranteed production of its tamperproof bottle caps, a highly technical operation that required a doubling of the capitalization of the plant. The International Union of Electrical Workers unionized the plant in 1976, and it was the only plastics firm that was organized. We were told that the unionization was successful despite the threats of layoffs and plant closings because the company eliminated Blue Cross medical coverage, crossing the line of acceptable management relations.

Greylock Plastics was later closed by the company in 1986. The selling of the kin-based industries local concerns to outside corporations is a new phenomenon and points to the tension in the ideology of the owners. The larger firms were subject to unionization by its workers, who, despite the lack of alternatives, reacted to the low wages and benefits offered. The separation of workers and owners introduces the standard categories of class struggle, that of workers and management. Once paternalistic ties in the workplace no longer function to provide a family atmosphere, the commitment on the part of the workers to maintain production lessens. Like Warner and Low's Yankee City, the community realizes the loss of its own power when locally based concerns are sold to outside corporations. This process becomes more acute as competition from abroad undercuts the stability of the market. Asked if he thought the era of firm generation by family ties was coming to an end, one manager told me:

> I think to a large extent, I don't think it can be what it used to be.
> . . . It's too tough. Financing is tough, just getting the work is
> hard, you know, the conditions are not there anymore, there will
> still be people who'll try it. . . . I think that we're all vulnerable
> now. You take Polymatrix, George Rufo, he's done a hell of a job
> with that whole thing, started out as Lakewood, and from there,
> Poly and Syntronics and a couple more, but I think that the product that he is involved with is proprietary, and I think he's vulnerable to being undercut, you know from abroad or wherever. I
> have to give George a lot of credit, he's done a lot of great things
> over there and seems to be continuing to do them.

General Electric Plastics

The plastics operation at General Electric sharply contrasted with that of the small plastics firms, reflecting the uneven development characteristic between the multinational and the local economy. The new international plastics headquarters looms over Plastics Avenue, built from steel, Lexan, and glass on land that could not be excavated for Indian artifacts because of the dangerous levels of contamination found in the soil. The $5 million building was designed as a sales tool. Joseph G. Wirth, general manager of GE plastics technology, told a *Berkshire Eagle* reporter that "We wanted a building that would look distinctive. . . . GE is a world leader in thermoplastics development and [the technology center] has to *look* like a world headquarters and express the state of the technical art" (July 24, 1984). The corporation hired a local artist with a national reputation to design a large sculpture for the atrium, an 8½ by 6 foot piece made from GE Lexan and aluminum, steel, and neon lights. The atrium of the 125,000 square foot building is roughly the size of most of the smaller plastics firms. It is designed to look like it houses the work performed there—the research and design strategies accomplished with computer simulations and telecommunications.

The invention of Lexan in 1953 revolutionized the plastics industry and catapulted General Electric to the top of the field in international plastics technology. General Electric plastics production in Pittsfield had been deteriorating during the 1940s, prompting the employment of an efficiency expert in 1948. It is said that the "local definition of an optimist at that time was a GE plastics worker who brought his lunch to work." The expert reorganized the business and sold off the moldmaking and molded plastics operations, displacing almost 1,000 workers. John F. Welch Jr. was then the head of the plastics division. The subsequent success of its international marketing propelled him up the corporate ladder to chief executive officer, a post he has held since 1981. In 1983, the plastics division accounted for over one billion dollars in sales, or 8 percent of GE's total market. Under the new plastics manager, Glen Hiner, General Electric opened new plants in Japan and the Netherlands in 1982 and acquired an Australian affiliate.

David Noble (1979) has described the process of technological innovation by which research and development is performed in major technological centers and then transferred to areas with lower labor costs for production. A major focus of the research phases of the production of new materials is the deskilling aspect noted by Braverman (1974). At the same time that General Electric was expanding its research development efforts, the company opened up GE Plastics Japan, formed a joint venture in Mexico, and expanded its facilities in Bergen op Zoom, the Netherlands, for production of the materials. The worldwide expansion of GE plastics prompted some observers to predict "a renaissance in the Berkshires" and the *Berkshire Eagle* quoted Herb Rammath, vice president and general manager of the Plastic Sales Division, predicting that "because we are both on the cutting edge of the future both in terms of plastic research and applications development, our facility will attract to the Berkshires moldmakers, design engineers, and the end users of plastics from all over the world" (September 1, 1984). Rammath failed to mention the concentration of moldmakers and design engineers already in the Berkshires and the difference between plastics and the electronics production that has been built up around Boston and the Silicon Valley. As Snow (1982) points out, the success of Silicon Valley is largely due to the fact that a large percentage of the electronics industry's products are purchased by the United States military and by law must be produced in the United States. Also, unlike plastics, electronics technology changes rapidly and requires close contact between engineers and producers.

The existence of the Plastics Technology Center has not produced the groundswell of industrial immigration hoped for. Because the corporation has contracted outside of the community for the testing of its resins and molds, local industry did not reap the benefit promised by General Electric planners and development specialists. Moreover, local manufacturers could adapt the technology being created at the center only if there was capital to use it. Commenting on the differences in the level of technology applied by the corporation and local firms, one manufacturer told us:

> How do we take advantage of today's technology? It would probably cost me a million, a minimum of a million to put out a CAD/CAM [computer assisted design/computer assisted manufacturing] system, to put in the machinery to take advantage of that, then with no guarantees that I'm going to have enough work to make this thing pay. Especially when you're sitting here, waiting for some engineer over at GE who's playing with this computer to develop a part, and meanwhile the payments keep coming in, and you know, so really its challenge for the small guy, how do you cope with it.

Development Efforts and the Plastics Industry

There was widespread frustration on the part of plastics entrepreneurs concerning the role of state and city planners in development efforts. Most felt that they were invisible in planning strategies and complained that a numerical code did not even exist for their businesses in the state's lexicon of manufacturing industries. Concerned about the importation of plastic molds from abroad, a group of the shop owners went to the Commerce Department for import statistics, only to discover that there none existed. As one of the men told us, "There was nothing, absolutely nothing on plastic molds, being imported, going out. . . . Where the hell is the data? Well, it was with the rubber molds, we're lumped in with the rubber industry, and we have nothing to do with the rubber industry." Many felt that city managers were insensitive to their needs, concerned more with abstract concepts of attracting industry rather than helping local concerns expand their own facilities. Commenting on the local efforts, one moldmaker complained "that's another thing that bugs me about [their] economic development approach. I don't think it would bother people who are doing it at all to bring another firm in to compete with [us], maybe even put [us] out of business at some point. I don't think that would bother them too much. They're looking at employment, and to me that's not right."

The growth of the plastics industry in Pittsfield began to slow in 1983 after a boom period of twenty-five years. While in the late 1980s and 1990s it began to grow again, the industry experiences the downturns that are characteristic of small firms with minimal local support. When I asked one of the "second-generation" owners how the industry had changed, he told me:

> Well, you know historically, at least in this area, you get a couple of guys who work next to each other in a shop and they get talking, and say hey, let's start our own shop, and they would do it, and in three or four years, they'd have 10, 12 maybe 15 people working for them, and they're off and running. But no more, the last two guys who did that are still two guys still struggling, in fact one of them is working without medical benefits, so they are not booming by any means. But what the offshore thing has done is not only going abroad, but it's made domestic competition much fiercer. Now even in the Midwest it's like that. You've got a shrunken piece of pie and everyone is going after that piece, so it ripples right down.

When I told him that I had heard the biggest competition was coming from Portugal, he continued:

> It depends on what area you're talking about. Around here it seems to be Portugal. The fact of the matter is if it wasn't Portugal it'd be somebody else and after Portugal it will be someone else, so it's something that's going to keep going on. You've got Korea, you've got Taiwan, it's going on forever, you've got half the continent of Africa starving to death right now and someday they're going to come on board and all of China that's still fumbling around, so to me, there are very many fundamental problems that I don't think politicians in this country are addressing themselves to.

Dissatisfaction with the way in which development was addressed by the city led to the formation of the Plastics Association under the auspices of the Chamber of Commerce. The director of the association said:

> I organized it. It was just that there seemed to be a need to promote the industry not only to make people in the area aware of what they had, but to try to promote ourselves as an industry outside the area. And I think what really did it in a big way was the impact of offshore sourcing on us. Up until five years ago, plastics was a real growth industry. We didn't have to sell much. We didn't have to do much marketing, they were pounding on our doors. All the sudden that stopped.

The uneven development of production between General Electric and the local industries was aptly summed up by the same informant:

> People here are still locked into the 1950s type thinking. In that back then you went into a shop and you had a row of machines and a guy looking at the machines says this business is booming. You might be looking at a company that's going down the tubes. The thing of it is, that if you're in a business that's labor intensive, then you're probably going to be heavily impacted by offshore sourcing. There is nothing, to me, from reading different periodicals, and from just being, there's nothing in manufacturing today that calls for more people, the whole trend is less people. *Automation.* Your big companies, they either automate or they go offshore. One or the other. When it comes right down to the small guy, if you cannot become more efficient machinerywise, then you're in big trouble.

This company was able to automate some production, but was forced to live with another ever present contradiction: while supplies of minimum wage labor has been plentiful, the demand for skilled moldmakers and engineers far outpaces supply. He was forced to resign as the director of the Plastics Association because of the resignation of one of his key employees, who left to join another company. "With him gone I've got to put my apron back on and go back onto the floor, I just cannot devote the time to these other things."

There was a good deal of hostility toward General Electric as a result of the corporation's indifference toward local firms. Because the Plastics Association was organized through the Chamber of Commerce, which had General Electric as its most prominent member, the attempts to initiate association meetings was met with resistance by Chamber members. The wariness of the shop owners toward the Chamber and its orientation was evident in their lack of active participation. Describing a development function that he planned with the Chamber and General Electric, the Plastic Association's director related the following:

> I think that out of 20 firms, and these were just for plastics, out of 20 firms, 13 responded and 3 of us showed up. At let me tell you, I was one of the three and I was embarrassed, and mad, and if there had been a hole big enough I would have crawled into it. But I know the people who are in this industry and they don't deserve to do that to themselves. People who were there, these were noted people in the community, and they were saying who are you people, we put something on like this, and you don't respond, and when you do, you still don't show up, and I thought, we don't

deserve to do that to ourselves. And that's what got me to write a letter and to start to organize this thing.

The Chamber of Commerce created a special section for small business. It was chaired by the proprietor of a small monument-making business who maintained a cheery outlook on Pittsfield's economy and the place of GE in development efforts. When I mentioned that we spoke with the director of the Chamber and that he commented that the community was much more positive than the last time we interviewed him, she responded:

Well, you know, sometimes a community becomes aware of what's happening considerably later than it actually has begun to happen. So that while the trend was upward a year and a half ago, people really were not aware of that, and they were pessimistic, extremely pessimistic, the whole economy was down as far as the people were feeling, and that was true for small business, and all business, and GE too.

The chair was raised in Boston and came to the area as an administrative aid to Congressman Silvio Conti. She said that it was while working with him that she became interested in the fate of small businesses and was made directly responsible for decisions affecting that sector. When I asked her how she thought the area had changed, she voiced the ideology of the Chamber and other outside-oriented visionaries with a particularly poignant perspective:

Well, I think its been an awful lot of work on everyone's part. And . . . it's taken a lot of growth and development and maturity on the part of individuals to, recognize that it is a bigger world out there. Its been very insular. I can remember when I first came here, there were people who had never left Pittsfield, you know a trip to Dalton [an adjoining town] was an adventure, and I think it was a very secure and pleasant community, and I think probably always has been, but it's taken awhile to realize—to update it. . . . There is an invasion happening, and its interesting because the local people are aware of this. There is an invasion from New York City that has really affected the areas around Pittsfield. . . . You're finding farm property going for a hundred thousand dollars that used to go for a thousand dollars for twenty acres. And all of a sudden people in Pittsfield are saying, "What is happening around us?" And it is happening, and it is very real.

While almost 500 of the 700 members of the Chamber are small businesses, the small business committee consisted of twelve individuals who plan functions and organize meetings. Many of the meetings were jointly sponsored by GE and the flavor of the committee suggested an orientation coming from the corporation. When I asked her about the outlook for Pittsfield's development, she replied:

> I think Pittsfield is a fairly solidly based community, and if you're doing a small hardworking business, you do well here. I think Pittsfield is hesitant to accept entrepreneurs, they need to be convinced that this is a good firm, but all those moldmakers that spun off from GE and so on, we have local people that have started on a shoestring and have done extremely well, and now they're taking on work which is far beyond the local level, but they work very hard, and they were all very well trained, this is what is very interesting. There is a lot of skill in Pittsfield, the training that GE did that actually is to the advantage of other firms, the trends in the plastics firms, the mold firms, the computer services, is reflected in the strength of the insurance companies, the number of lawyers that are doing business, the number of bankers, its an asset to the community.

> *How do insurance companies become a reflection?*
> Just because the businesses abound, and don't forget with a small business, just to exist it must have certain kinds of insurance, a lot.

This section leader thought that there was an unfair distinction in the community between big and small business and that the mistrust of large business was unjustified. From the Chamber's point of view, business attracts business and large facilities feed small facilities. While her position in the Chamber induced her to view General Electric and big business generally in a favorable light, the lack of success in attracting another large industry to the Berkshires forced her to voice support for those in favor of concentrating on locally based growth, in name if not in deed. Her statements often came back to the issue of making the state more attractive to outside industry—a position favored by General Electric because of the tax abatements it implies.

The decline of industry is internalized by the shop owners as a problem of attitude as much as it is blamed on the contingencies of offshore sourcing and the planning perspectives of those responsible for local development efforts. The self-blame internalized by community residents is in line with one of Arensberg's "Assumptions of American Culture" (1956): the association of failure on the part of individuals when jobs cannot be found or endeavors do not succeed. Unlike England, for example, where employment is viewed as a right rather than a privilege and the failure of small industries is rooted in the class relations of the country, Americans tend to see themselves as the cause of disappointing results. The director of the Plastics Association described the lack of statistics by commenting that "the fact that like Berkshire County where we employ about 1,200 people, and pump about $20 million into the economy a year, and Marland Mold over there is probably one of the most sophisticated tool shops in the country and they don't know that. This is a strength in the community and they don't even know that. A lot of it is our fault." The problem, as he saw it, involved the same qualities of the community that allowed the firms to thrive: the secrecy and dependency and self-reliant pride that was a hallmark of the industry. At the time fieldwork was done, the same entrepreneurs who refused to be dependent on General Electric for their livelihood also resisted organizing for lobbying efforts. General Electric was a member of the association, but had not paid its dues.

Corporate and Community Ideology in the Development of Industry

Jack Welch made his name in the industry by raising profits and eliminating jobs. In the same year that the Plastics Technology Center was announced, creating twenty professional jobs, Genel closed its doors and dislodged over a hundred workers.

Unlike community organizations and associations, the ideology of the corporation was direct and intact. In 1986, 112 corporate officers were called in to comment on a draft of company values, drafted by Welch and entitled *Where We Want to Be*. In it, Welch stated that the corporation's businesses would have to maintain first or second place in their markets or be closed down, and he suggested that employees who were not comfortable with the company's values should find work elsewhere (*Business Week*, June 30, 1986). Welch's open insistence that profits be placed above all other concerns produced pressure on managers that generated a number of scandals, including an accusation by the federal government that General Electric knowingly overcharged the Defense Department in 1980. Locally, the company has been involved with debates over pollution. The corporation's lack of commitment to the community is not fully comprehended by the residents who depend on their past experiences to interpret present circumstances. It is better understood by the small companies who see work that could be performed locally farmed out to other regions and countries. The discrepancy inherent in formal planning policy was aptly summed up in a statement by the Plastics Association president, who noted that at the same time General Electric was moving production offshore, local retired executives were being used to train and organize foreign small industries:

> What happens with GE, is that they just look at their dollars and
> cents and their numbers, and if that means the cost is going to

effect the product then maybe that product is going to go offshore. Losing jobs. It seems that people in government today, the politicians, the left hand doesn't know what the right hand is doing. Nobody knows the cause and effect of things. Here's a good example. [Shows me a brochure by the Organization of Retired Executives.] It's a function of our foreign policy. They're funded by AID, which is a government-funded organization, and they do good work throughout the country. . . . Here's an example. "Mr. Ellis in Lumnister, Massachusetts, advises a toy manufacturer in dyes and molds for the Korean Trade Manufacturer's Association in Seoul. As an IECS volunteer Mr. Ellis aided the client in all areas of moldmaking for plastics." Great. Don't they know what they're doing? What does this mean for us here? Don't these people know the cause and effect of what they're doing? . . . It probably helps GE because they can get cheap tools built overseas.

The Chamber of Commerce fought for and convinced the city to grant a large tax abatement for the technology center—an act that awed even Jack Welch. Local residents understood the contradiction between the city's efforts and their own commitment in terms of values instilled by ethnic communities and encouraged by GE's past behavior. One new shop owner described it in this way: "[Our view] is primarily from our New England ideology, the way we were brought up, taught to live, taught to experience, and taught to love what we are doing, where we are and who we are and the work ethic that is instilled in us—work hard, push ahead, just keep on working."

CHAPTER 8

Economic Development and Social Responsibility

A Case Study

Common sense tells us that the outcome of productive work is the provision of human needs. Unfortunately, excepting a small portion of the population for whom profit is deemed needed, this is generally not so. Under capitalism, corporate entities exist for profit. What they produce depends on the market that they often manipulate, creating consumer needs through advertising or linked product development. When the market is good and "corporate citizenship" is operating in full swing, issues of health, housing, and education are part of the social good. As corporations, however, seek to increase their profit margins or find themselves differing with the communities and workers who make their products, social welfare is discarded in favor of hard-line economics.

Economic downturns have social consequences. Human needs are not priority items in the planning meetings of corporate entities, and as we have witnessed in the United States, the social net disappears when profit becomes the primary motive.

But the profit motive affects more than the objective structure of social services. The scientific principles used to detect the etiology of presenting problems are also influenced by modes of analysis that place profit before human well-being. The present controversy over health care and managed plans is a concrete example of profit over health. Speed and anonymity prevail where cost is a predominant concern. Another is the discourse over corporate by-products and toxic waste, the disposal of harmful substances, and the corrective action needed to appropriately mediate between corporate, community, and individual interests.

It has become a mainstay in America today that health problems are in the realm of the individual rather than the corporate world. This parallels the American cultural fascination with the individual, who is, as Arensberg (1956) discussed, responsible for the upswings and downturns of life's circumstances. Diseases that are suspiciously linked to substances used or discarded by corporate bodies are more often attributed to the behavioral characteristics of the individuals who are unfortunate enough to have contacted them. Lifestyle attributes, whether they be smoking, eating, or genetic malfunctions, explain the presence of diseases and take precedence over environmental factors that implicate corporate participation. The corporations producing these substances, for the most part, justify their actions by the promise of job loss and competitive disadvantage that would accompany responsibility. While the "tobacco is not addictive" argument is an extreme form of this, many other, subtler forms of denial of with the consequences of production are used by corporate entities in the mad rush to sustain high margins of profit.

In Pittsfield, the corporate maneuvering over responsibility for corporate by-products had concrete meaning. During the 1980s, controversies over issues of health arose concerning the levels of PCBs produced in Pittsfield and being released into Pittsfield's air. Higher levels than would be expected of cancer and other life-threatening diseases were noticed by community members, but denied by corporate and city managers.

The Health Crisis in Pittsfield

The health crisis that occurred in Pittsfield concerned the discovery of toxic wastes and a fear in the community that the incidence of cancer among friends and neighbors appeared to be rising at an alarmingly high rate. The differences between corporate and community approaches to this issue produced a schism that was not witnessed since the last major strike in 1969. Because the issue did not involve worker organization against General Electric, however, it was mediated with public relations tactics that appealed to logic presented and justified by the tenets of scientific thought controlled by corporate strategists. The worry that the community would be responsible for cleanup efforts combined with the reluctance to confirm suspicions about toxic wastes contributed to the acceptance of corporate ideology. Employees who were the most exposed to the toxic substances used in their work were the least likely to take action, particularly if they still worked in the plant.

The disjuncture in Pittsfield took shape in the early 1980s after large amounts of polychlorinated biphenyls (PCBs) were discovered in residential basements and sewer lines. PCBs were leftover wastes from the production of the power transformers, the mainstay of production in Pittsfield until the mid-1970s. The PCBs were part of a compound that comprised pyranol, a fire-resistant insulating agent used in the production of, and sealed inside, power transformers.

Contamination in a neighborhood adjacent to the plant was discovered in 1977, when pools of the substance were found in three basements and a bakery. General Electric quickly bought and demolished the houses, placing "No Trespassing" signs on the landscaped mounds of dirt that were used to cover over any evidence on the sites. Also concerned about issues being raised in New York State, where it had been discovered that PCBs had contaminated large sections of the upper Hudson River, General Electric quietly took the position that it would buy any houses where PCBs were discovered.

The community became concerned in 1980 when news of the substance in basements became known and residents of the Lakewood neighborhood witnessed crews making test digs on their streets. One of the residents described her reaction to the digging:

> One day that started drilling on Lombard Street which is right over here. The men were around, and you know, if you see a gas company truck, you think they must be putting in a gas line, or if you see an electric company truck, they're putting electric in, or whatever. It so happened, that two or three people, not knowing what was going on, said "What is this?" I was going out myself one day, and I said to one of the workers, "What are you doing?" No answer. That's crazy. I said "I hope it's not gas or it will blow up my house." He said, 'I don't know.' That's how it started. When anyone asked any questions, they didn't answer. We went directly to Ray.

Ray Del Gallo, a former mayor of Pittsfield, was a resident of the neighborhood. Known for his outspoken manner, he owned a popular neighborhood Italian restaurant where the workers drilling the test digs went to eat. When he asked them what they were doing, the drillers said that they were checking the water level. But the drilling of 200 wells raised suspicions. After talking with public relations officials at the company, Del Gallo discovered that the tests had uncovered PCB residues in eighteen residential gardens and in twenty cellars. The company later put dyes into the pipes that discharged wastes into the lake behind the plant, obviously looking for the source of the contamination. Ray commented that

I went over and told them, "I'm going to be cooperative and show you some places where you dumped the stuff, You're talking with a native!" They didn't appreciate that. All along the river bank are dump sites: Merrill Road down New York Avenue—when you have a heavy downpour, that stuff all just goes into the river. And they wonder where it comes from! I took them to a place on Newell Street where there were hundreds of barrels. I said, "If you doubt me, I'll bring you the individuals who dumped it!"

Ray continued:

You see there above the railroad? General Electric used to have tanks with a capacity of 275,000 gallons. Those tanks leaked oil for years—since the early thirties. When the trains used to go by, you could see the oil squishing up under the wheels. But they say we have no problem! In the old days, they used to bring in grapes in those oil tanks for the people to make wine.

The State Department of Environmental Quality Engineering (DEQE) entered the investigation shortly after the finding of PCBs, as is required by Massachusetts law. In examining samples from the Housatonic River, the Lakewood area, and East Street, the company found more PCB traces than the state did. The DEQE spokespersons agreed with the corporation that most of the oil that leaked from underground storage tanks on GE grounds was isolated in a "plume" on the GE side of East Street. An executive committee was formed with representatives of city government, including the mayor, the health commissioner, the executive director of the Berkshire County Regional Planning Association, and residents of the Lakewood neighborhood.

The residents acted early on the contamination. When we asked Ray Del Gallo about the deliberations of the committee, he told us that

The consulting firm that handled Love Canal was called in. The vice-president told us that it was fortunate for us that the oil flowed along that plume instead of following the water line. But we were afflicted no matter what he said about the miracle plume. We fought them all the way, since we are the natives. We have our own contacts in Boston. I have a cousin who is an engineer and knows the language. We went to a law firm in Boston with Representative Shelsy, a top law firm in the field of toxic wastes. And we fought with them in the council.

When the issue was raised in the council, Del Gallo showed up with a bucket of oil containing PCBs that he had taken from the basement of a bakery in Lakewood. The consultants asserted that there was little danger from the PCBs because the land in Lakewood was so closely knit that it wouldn't penetrate. But as Ray pointed out to them, "Lakewood was called Lakewood for a reason: when there are floods, that miracle plume floods also and the entire area is covered with it."

The Cost Accounting Approach

General Electric planning is guided by rates of profit. Their numbers are defined by strategies developed at corporate headquarters in Fairfield, Connecticut and do not include community information. Jack Welch declared in 1981 that divisions of the corporation that did not perform first or second in their competitive field would be closed down eliminating 100,000 jobs from the company's payrolls during his first year in office.

The ongoing concern in the Pittsfield community was that General Electric would decide that all of its divisions there were not profitable enough to continue operations since direct challenges to the corporation by the community were historically met with vague or implied threats to relocate or close down. City administrators mediate discussion between the corporation and community groups, and where possible, procure the concessions needed to stabilize the relationship. Where unresolvable conflicts of interest appeared, city managers publically defined their role in relation to state and federal agencies in an attempt to reduce conflict that could develop into schisms between the corporation and the dependent community.

General Electric stated its role to the community in repeated references to economic necessity. Where implied threats were not enough to placate pockets of dissatisfaction, the corporation relied on more sophisticated levels of ideology that included the manipulation of law and science.

The case of a conflict over environmental contamination in Pittsfield illustrates the way in which an ideology defines the direction of negotiation. In scientific discourse, often wedded to corporate funding and channeled by environmental agencies influenced by political appointees, any impending sense of danger among residents was subsumed and negated under skillfully manipulated statistics. Given the intimate connections with that part of the scientific establishment that carries out studies of risk related to industrial operations, the government agencies that set rules and standards based on those studies, and the corporations that monitor and often fund such research, industry spokespeople are one step ahead of their critics while they simultaneously subvert any discussion of recognized danger.

Thus the fear that a danger exists and the action necessary to stem potential damage is moderated by the corporation in a way that places costs above human consequences. The ideology is formulated and disseminated by the needs and structure of corporations that make decisions based on capital accumulation and expansion. The realities of potential danger are translated into cost accounting principles—costs of cleanup and retribution are compared with rates of profit and reconciled with jobs and corporate investment. The approach maintains that humanitarian concerns about employment, health hazards, and the survival of the community are subservient to the dictates of the market, as defined by the corporation.

The primacy of profits despite human costs has become the core of an amoral modus operandi. In an issue of *Science*, Daniel A. Koshland coined the phrase the "undesirability principle," concluding that relative costs should be adjusted to include corporate desires to dump toxic wastes at the lowest possible cost, environmental group demands to place severe restraints on dumping, and consumer desires to obtain products at the lowest costs available. He proposes that the principle be enacted by a law that requires protagonists to state clearly to society the undesirable aspects of their proposal.[1]

Koshland's principle does not acknowledge the profound differences in the degree to which different populations are subjected to the hazards of toxic substances in the workplace and in the home, or the relations of power that define those differences. Production workers immediately exposed to harmful substances are equated in the analysis with the executives who sit at their desks. People of moderate or low incomes do not have the same access to health testing and care that those with substantial incomes enjoy.

Community Response and Corporate Responsibility

From the beginning of the investigation, General Electric played down the significance of the problem. A spokesman for the Office of Community Relations at General Electric responded to our questions by stating that

> In Lakewood, there is a well-defined, tight-knit community bounded by the river when the people began talking that GE had underground storage leaking PCBs. We did tests and were well satisfied that they remained on the east side. There we found several cellars above the FTA limits. We offered to clean up some more. Some people felt that they lost real estate value. Some have had difficulty selling their houses, so we bought three of them. You've got to take what they say with a grain of salt. I've been amazed how many will say they remember when they put in so and so many drums at a certain place, and when you ask them to go down and show you, they can't find anything. I eat Housatonic fish.

Those who work with it have elevated levels of PCBs. The highest level in Pittsfield was 200-300 level. In the city council, they issued a consent agreement. I went down there to discuss it with them. I asked my doctor what the danger of 200 PCB level was, and they had no idea of the significance. We talk about it with the proper amount of respect.

When the environmental chief at the plant was told that hazardous materials, including PCBs and arsenic, were found in a landfill site in the summer of 1980, he joked that "I looked at some 400 drums at the dump. It's an exotic occupation. Some I took out because of some intellectual curiosity about them." The company quitely initiated an epidemiological study in 1979, funding researchers from the Harvard School of Public Health after they had independently noted a higher than average rate of cancer among General Electric workers in Pittsfield.

The concern voiced by the corporation, and repeated by the researchers during the course of the study, was the quality of the data and the validity of impressions voiced by the community. Corporate policy was responding to worries voiced not only by community members, but by its own employees. Attempts to diffuse the distress started as early as 1969,[2] when the corporation circulated a manuscript by an engineer in the Schenectady plant, who wrote

> Our knowledge of chlorinated biphenyl formulations and possible deleterious effects is not as complete as is desirable in today's climate of concern for maintaining and improving the quality of life in its environmental aspects, with regard to worker protection, and in terms of product safety. Nevertheless, it is not responsible to suggest that "other materials be substituted" until all doubts are resolved. It must be remembered that virtually all applications of Pyranol are the end product of intensive research directed toward finding the best material for the application, that substitution would involve tradeoffs, not only with performance factors and other economic factors, but with product safety considerations themselves—i.e., flammability and explosion possibilities.[3]

General Electric declared that it was better suited than others to judge product safety and therefore potential danger, despite increasing evidence that PCBs were causing health problems around the globe.

A follow-up report of the victims of a Japanese incident, where villagers consumed rice contaminated with PCBs, showed an excess in the rate of cancer, particularly of the stomach and liver (*USA Today*, 1980). A study done at Mount Sinai Hospital in New York found that workers who "swallowed, inhaled or absorbed the chemical" experienced skin disease, jaundice, and liver damage (Fischbein et al., 1983). The New York Academy of Sciences reported that workers exposed to PCBs showed a decreased vital capacity similar to workers who were exposed to asbestos, manifested in eye and upper respiratory irritations and tightness in the chest (1979). By the mid-1980s, even the popular press was referring to PCBs as cancer-causing substances.

Pittsfield's Lakewood residents and the workers directly exposed to PCBs became increasingly alarmed about the effects of the substance on their health. When we asked a Lakewood resident whether she thought people got sick from PCBs, she replied:

> I think if I'm not mistaken, they have a suit going on because we've been talking an awful lot about cancer in this area. . . . [W]e older, we people that have been here a long time could tell you that in almost every house, someone died of cancer. Now they don't want to hear about it. They say that in any other city, the percentage is just as much.

She continued:

> My mother was 61 years old. She had cancer. Across the street, the older ones, one of them had cancer. The next house was the Magis. He had cancer. He's fine right now, but he was in his early thirties when he got it. The next house over there, there's a woman upstairs who also had, well, Lil has had a lot of things the matter with her, really a lot of things. Downstairs, the man has cancer at the moment. He's almost 57 or 58 years old. . . . The colon seems to be the most affected. We all had a tremendous scare. We all had gardens here. The majority of everyone down here is Italian, and behind every house there is a garden. Its part of the house.

While residents of the neighborhood were noting an increase in sickness, a retired engineer at the plant, Ed Bates, began quantifying cancer-related deaths with those workers who had direct contact with pyranol. As part of management, he tried to work with the company in proving that there was a correlation, but was then dismissed with a "golden handshake" and treated as a quack by members of his union, who attributed his activity to boredom associated with early retirement. Yet Bates's concern was motivated by his feelings that he was responsible for these deaths, and his willingness to fight brought results. He told us that

> The guys who worked for me, and I remember this, they were saying, "Jesus, I'm getting headaches and I don't feel good." And I'd say, "Look, I sympathize with you, but there's nothing in the GE

records that say that this is bad. You have got to apply for another job." And they go down maybe five steps and 60 cents an hour, the union couldn't help them. The union says, "Hey, we're going strictly by seniority, you got to go down to the bottom if you want another job." So the guys would stay out there (in testing). I was essentially sending guys to their death.

Able to convince the influential retirees group of his findings, they supported him with more data. The group began to put together their knowledge of who had worked with the substance and who was sick and who died. They found that those who had worked on repairs where the PCB-laden oils spilled out on them as they reassembled the transformers seemed especially liable.

The sustained efforts resulted in an allocation directed from Senator Ted Kennedy to study environmental contamination and health problems in Pittsfield. Blood tests were taken from volunteer community residents by the University of Massachusetts, which found that while work at General Electric was highly correlated with blood PCB levels, residence in the Lakewood neighborhood did not correlate in higher levels than those of residents in other areas. A later Massachusetts COSH study showed PCB levels in Lakewood fifteen times that of the general population: the average level was 20 or 30 parts per billion while their sample of 43 General Electric workers found 9 with more than 100 and 3 over 300.

The Social Construction of Science

General Electric responded to the research by emphasizing the "complexity" of the problem and the potential consequences of "precipitous" action. Corporate spokespeople took a noticeably harder line toward the issue as demands for action grew in the community. As Ray Del Gallo reported,

> When the former heads of relations were here (before 1982 when many left because of the downscaling of production in the power transformer division) they sat down with us, discussed problems and offered to buy property if people were uneasy, although they kept telling us that there was no danger. Now with the new management over there, they are playing hardball. "Your property is not a problem," they say, "We don't want to hear about it."

A GE spokesperson with whom we spoke in 1982 similarly downplayed the role of PCBs as an occupational or environmental health problem:

Our experience in nearly forty years of use here in Pittsfield is similar to medical records over the country during the period. This record shows that the only adverse health effect experienced by workers exposed to PCBs have been limited to occasional skin irritations which clear up quickly.

The epidemiological study that was commissioned by General Electric in 1979 was repeatedly delayed by requests for more information and claims of insignificant findings. A major area pursued by the researchers and the corporation was the effects of other health factors on cause-of-death statistics. The tactic by the corporation to separate health issues from work experience served to segment and narrow the field in which health risks could be viewed. The point that workers spent most of their waking life in a plant setting where hazardous materials were present and went home in environments also contaminated by waste materials became easily overshadowed by the presence of individual risk factors such as smoking and problems with weight control.

Ed Bates and an associate from the testing division continued to encourage legislators to act on the issue of the research and, in 1987, succeeded in convening a meeting with a state representative, the head of the National Institute of Occupational Safety and Health (NIOSH), General Electric officials, and the principal investigator of the study, Dr. David Wegman. The meeting was scheduled and then cancelled by GE, not to be rescheduled until the state representative threatened to have the federal government audit the data. At the meeting, Ed Bates and his associate presented their case concerning a special study of Buildings 12 and 100, where final assembly of power transformers took place. These were the sites of maximal exposure to PCBs, as well as to solvents, benzene, asbestos, and machining fluids. A list they compiled showed 85 deaths from cancer in Buildings 12 and 100, 62 of those in Building 12, where men in testing worked directly with PCBs. In Dr. Wegman's review of these buildings, he used information supplied by GE and found only 36 cancer victims in the list of 173 deaths of long-term employees of Building 12. When we asked Bates about the discrepancies in the data sets, he told us that

> I think that there have been certain exclusions from the data—that modify the results. The thing that bothers Charlie and me is that they've had all this data and everything for four and a half years and they haven't included them. One of the reasons that they said they didn't include all those who have died is that four or five of them were from North Adams or Adams, and they died up there at Fairview Hospital. Then there was one from Savoy and two from Great Barrington, but all these were people that worked in this

area. But they had worked for me for 15 or 20 years. That's when we drove them into the wider study for Berkshire County. There were 168 codes on their list of people working in Building 12, and there were only 15 of those codes actually working there. All the others were from Ordnance or something, and they were pouring them all into Building 12 to dilute the whole. The GE's got billions and billions of dollars, and they do down and give this story to the medical people. I'm not saying its incorrect, but its adulterated so that it looks fine.

Bates's claim that the researcher's data included workers who had never been assigned to the designated buildings was never resolved. The director of NIOSH expressed outrage that the data sets were not reconciled and demanded that a recheck be made. Convinced by the state representative (who also chaired the legislative committee charged with funding research) to incorporate Bates's data into his own, Dr. Wegman later rejected General Electric's assertion that his study was flawed by the way that risk assessment had been assigned to each job.

In October 1987, Dr. Wegman was invited to speak at a dinner party that included the Pittsfield medical establishment. About seventy-five doctors came to the Pittsfield Country Club, where General Electric's medical director, Harold Stein, introduced the talk by joking that he was going to sue GE for breach of contract for the delay in the results of the study was holding up his retirement. Dr. Wegman explained how the data records were compiled:

> We were able to come up with about two-thirds of the work history records, with the major failures being in the earlier studies in 1969 at a period of time when there was no reason except inertia to keep the records of that type for people who were pensioned and left the company. So we went for those work records, and we did another analysis looking at major occupations during the lifetime. That gave us some additional clues. It also indicated that there was enough variability in the way that they were distributed, and some new confusions, so that we decided to go the full mile and address the question in the most comprehensive state-of-the-art way that we could. I think that's one of the strengths of the way the study is structured now. It's also one of the reasons why Harold is suing me for breach of contract.

Completed in 1987, six years after its scheduled release, the results concluded that PCBs had no significant effect on Pittsfield's population. Speaking at the General Electric Company's ordnance facility with the GE logo displayed prominently around the room, Dr. Wegman repeated in

October of 1987 that the number of specific kinds of cancer was too small to be statistically significant under recognized statistical procedure. Because of the statistical problems, Wegman reported, a concrete cause-and-effect statement might never be possible (*Berkshire Eagle* November, 1987). The problems with the data and the inferences drawn from statistical correlations became moot issues as conclusions were given the weight of scientific validity. At this stage, the onus of proof was on the victims since, based on the study, employees with cancer cannot make a claim that their illness is occupationally related. Simply stated, the ability to direct scientific inquiry toward proving that materials such as PCBs are hazardous, rather than that they are safe for human ecosystems, places the onus on the workers and the community—people affected by the hazard. Since few workers have the knowledge and background to undertake a study that would be accepted by the scientific community, and since the engineers and managers who do have sophisticated understanding of statistics are not legitimated by the academy, the present arrangement concerning the burden of proof is usually unworkable in local settings. Thus, at the time, the corporation was given another reprieve from extending medical coverage to its employees following their retirement.

Meanwhile, the story continues. A front-page story of the August 10, 1997 edition of the *Boston Globe* reports that "GE knew of Pittsfield 'liability' for years." Basing the story on internal documents obtained by the newspaper, it quotes George Wislocki, president of the Berkshire Natural Resources Council stating that 'This is a cover-up, and it's been going on for a long time. Of Course GE knew about this, and I think even more sites will be identified'" (*Boston Globe*, August 10, 1997, p. 1). By 1996, when the internal documents were forwarded to the Department of Environmental Protection, the GE Plant was already a well-documented hazardous waste site. The EPA recommended in August, 1997 that the area be added to the Superfund list (*Boston Globe*, August 10, 1997, p. B5).

The Structure of Health Administration in Pittsfield

The importance of social welfare is directly correlated with the need for a healthy labor force. The structure of health care in Pittsfield worked against confronting major conflicts of interest between General Electric, which has a lessened need for labor, and the community, which needs jobs. Toxic wastes and other issues that significantly impact the community were relegated to state agencies that do not have a specific interest in the local population. Designating the Health Department as a minor agency within the structure of the city government acted to subvert claims by the community that inadequate public health care was being provided, while providing a disclaimer by city officials that they could influence or change policy regarding the community's relationship to General Electric.

Pittsfield has two major hospitals that service the area between Stockbridge and North Adams on one side, and Northampton on the other. Hillcrest Hospital, founded in 1908 as a voluntary, nonprofit, community hospital, is the smaller of the two institutions, which are active competitors for patients. The Berkshire Medical Center merged two hospitals in the early 1970s: Pittsfield General and the House of Mercy, the first combination of a religious and nonreligious hospital in the country. It is now the second largest employer in the area, far surpassing its competition in the number of hospital beds and ancillary services that include three nursing homes, a retirement care community, a proprietary laboratory mental health facility, and home care services. The hospital in 1988 completed a $3.5 million radiotherapy facility that was the result of a major fund-raising drive supported by Pittsfield's residents.

The hospital's role in public health is, as a senior administrator put it, "tangential":

> We operate a number of clinics, those kinds of things under the aegis of the Department of Public Health, but our work in this hospital is primarily acute care. I suppose that one can argue that some of the education programs that we put on, prenatal education and that kind of thing, begins to move in a public healthy kind of direction, but it isn't seen as a large part of our mission here.

The administrators and medical staff at the hospital were not involved in the PCB issue and did not focus on issues of potential conflict among interest groups in the community that it depends on for clientele and donations. The administrator I interviewed was concerned with the direction of the city's administration in economic development. He predicted that a further drop in population would jeopardize some of the programs the hospital operated and the recruitment of medical staff from New York and Boston. Stating that "the wind does change too often. This is crazy, absolutely crazy, you can't get anything done," the administrator worried that tension in the community would continue to work against a sound plan for economic development.

Public health in Pittsfield is regulated through the Office of the Commissioner of Public Health. There is a board of health whose members are either elected or appointed and an additional advisory board that sets agenda items for the monthly meetings. Statistical reports are compiled for annual publication. When we asked the health commissioner what his mandate was within the city government, he replied:

Very basically and briefly it is to be diligent for the health of the community in whatever way that means. Here in Pittsfield, our structure is a little different than other communities, our department also delivers school health services, so our, we have seven nurses and three part-time doctors, two dental hygienists, so we run standard programs, somewhat standard.

When we asked him how the department had changed over the years, and whether environmental issues were part of his purview, he continued:

There was a major change when I came on board. I've been here since 1959—I was late getting a college degree and thats when I graduated. In 1973 the commissioner at the time resigned, and he was a physician, so I was the major change at that time. City ordinances were changed to allow a nondoctor . . . most of the environmental checks that we do are governed by the state sanitary codes, and they were changed. That state health department used to have jurisdiction over most of our programs when I first started public health in 1959, over the years the state changed its structure, and the State Department of Environmental Quality Engineering was created, and they took several bones from the State Department of Public Health. . . . That for many years caused confusion, poor communication in local, and because there was a poor understanding in small communities with no staff, it caused no enforcement. . . . Now with the DEQE so much larger than it was in its infancy, and with its responsibility so much more than it was in its infancy, the staffing of programs hasn't caught up and it's just been growing so rapidly that they are having growing pains. And some of the results of that is miscommunication, and the regulations, we get so tied up in regulations that you don't know where you're turning.

Establishing the State Department of Environmental Quality Engineering had the opposite effect of its creators' intentions. Instead of providing an umbrella that could monitor industrial effects on the environment, the agency tied up complaints regarding potential hazards in bureaucratic scheming over turf. The city chose to stay out of the loop in the hope that potential conflicts would not further harm its relationship with General Electric. As the commissioner of economic development told us when asked about the responsibility for toxic waste cleanup,

In the case of GE property itself, they are being held accountable by the state and federal government. The city is simply attempting not to become a party that for some reason forces something to happen in a sequence that results in a major portion of the company leaving the community—because there are social consequences as well as environmental.

Thus, the bureaucracy of environmental control and the narrow scope of jobs in city and state government militates against these agents taking full responsibility for health problems in the environment. The administration of public health in Pittsfield suffered from the same crisis of leadership that governs the functioning of all aspects of city government. While the community is forced to walk the tightrope negotiated in the developing discourse between the corporation and government agencies, they have neither the resources nor the knowledge to play an effective role in changing the course of the policies that are developed within that framework. The denial of responsibility by the corporation, the business orientation of the medical infrastructure, and the fears that worked against any direct confrontation resulted in severely compromised public health activity in Pittsfield. There was no direct monitoring of the environment. Those individuals who did take on that responsibility were left to negotiate and fight the system without support. As Ed Bates lamented,

> The thing that really bothers me. . . . I know 4 or 5 guys that have died since and they exceeded their 90 days on Medicare where they got serum. They had to sell their houses and it took every cent they got. I get going on this. Some months my telephone bill is astronomical . . . and then you say, 'Hell, I'm going to give up.' . . . And you know, . . . you get so tired and beat and then I get mad at myself for quittin'.

The role of the environment in the city's struggle to restructure its economic base embodies the conflict among the community's sectors. Small business plans to expand were hampered by the possibility of contamination in areas where building was planned. The corporation's public position was one of support, while asking to be understood as a structure undergoing change because of its need to be responsive to a volatile economic environment. Privately, the change in focus has meant a negation of its responsibility for a situation that it has created, a claim that it no longer has responsibility for the community. The community has had to adapt to the changing role of the corporation by generating new sources of tax revenue and hoping that the public relations statements made by General Electric will help secure an economic future. While the administration of the city is divided and forced to respond to many different interest groups, the corporation is not. Chaos generated by the scrambling for revenue and directions for economic planning further weakens the city's position with the corporation, which can support its positions with the distribution of ideology that advertising budgets allow and subvent the full extent of the law when the ideology is challenged.

Gersuny (1981) sums up his analysis of *Work Hazards and Industrial Conflict* with the insight that differences in power and privilege go along with differences in the hazards to life and limb. The issues involved with toxic wastes are clearly demarcated by class lines and involve moral determinations by decision makers regarding the protection of human health.

Epilogue

John Nordheimer, in the the March 9, 1997 edition of the *New York Times* tells the story of a recently downsized mill town in Maine. Employees were accustomed to turnover in mill ownership and management over the last century, and, confident that their product, Sunbeam's electric blanket, had a stable market, most took the news of yet another change in ownership as par for the course. What they were not prepared for was the change in company tactics and ethics and the style of management that moved in, transforming the town's economic structure, which has been in place since the late nineteenth century.

The new chairman of the Sunbeam corporation had different ideas. As the *New York Times* reporter, John Nordheimer, wrote,

> Mr. Dunlap didn't get his nickname "Chainsaw Al" for nothing. In November, he announced that the Biddeford [Maine] plant would either shut down or be sold as part of his plan to slash Sunbeam's overall work force in half. When Robert B. Reich, then the nation's Labor Secretary, described the move as "treating employees as disposable pieces of equipment," Mr. Dunlap brushed off the criticism and said his first obligation was to the shareholders who hired him to make the company profitable. (March 9, 1997).

Nordheimer reported that the workers reacted to the news with disbelief, anger, and depression, but not acceptance. The dismay the employees felt was tied to their commitment to the community. Voicing the feelings of many, one employee commented that "we have the tradition, the experience, our families are here."

What happened in Biddeford in not unique. The Bureau of Labor Statistics reports that, on average, there are now ten plant closings per week in the United States, putting about 190 people out of jobs at each closing.

111

The tendency to nickname new chief executive officers for their ability to slash workforces and increase profits has become an American cultural artifact. It is accomplished in an almost endearing way, as if the actions taken by these hard-hitting executives are healthy signs of a progressive economy. Progressive for *whom* is rarely an issue as major stockholders and the company owners find themselves reaping the benefits of laying off workers. As one worker lamented, "Chainsaw Al doesn't care who he steps on and squashes, as long as he gets paid his millions."

Communities experiencing these transitions hope that a rescue will take place. Pittsfield continually based its future on the hope of new industry, or, better yet, the prospect that General Electric would see the light and maintain its presence. In Biddeford, hope is focusing on a local top-level Sunbeam executive who wants to see the plant remain open. In these cases hope correlates with luck.

When all else fails, chaos results. Similar to many towns and cities around the country, Lorain, Ohio, hit in early 1997 with the closing of its Thunderbird plant, remains in a state of disbelief. Likewise, Youngstown, Ohio, once a thriving auto-producing community, resembles a ghost town. Communities trying to cope with restructuring their economy on their own rarely have the experience or the resources to accomplish the task. Failure produces administrative and bureaucratic depression. As in newly independent states, city managers and community leaders who start out enthusiastically become disillusioned when progress is thwarted. Requests for information from the Pittsfield City Government are forgotten or go unanswered. The *Berkshire Eagle*, Pittsfield's once award winning-newspaper, was unresponsive to phone calls simply asking for copies of articles. If there is any productive use for the recent preoccupation with the analysis of "meaning" in the social sciences, it is for the explanation of this administrative depression. The explanation, of course, is primarily economic. But the lethargy that is the outcome also acts as substantiation for business leaders who complain that the community is not primed for development. While stores are abandoned in Pittsfield's downtown area in favor of the large retail mall, committees still debate alternative uses of vacant space and the attraction of outside industry without reaching consensus. The hope, by many, that the General Electric Corporation will provide leadership is still strong, despite evidence to the contrary. The subtext of disappointment and conflict with the corporation is symbolized by the public debates concerning parking restrictions at the plants, for both sides know that any substantial confrontation with General Electric will only engender threats to relocate remaining production and thus produce an even more insecure economic environment.

The similarity of positions taken by, in particular, the Chamber of Commerce, the General Electric Corporation, and the proponents of the modernization theory posited for the Third World during the 1950s and 1960s is striking. Modernization theory explains why development is not successful. Rather than look at the processes of uneven development that characterize a region, it is able to focus attention on individual resistance to capitalist expansion, blaming the victims for the failure of planning strategies and ignoring the relations of dependency that predominate.

Pittsfield's administrative community dealt with the chaos produced by corporate maneuvers by brainstorming about development efforts. Others, notably ex-GE workers allied with a strong Italian kinship network, branched out on their own to free themselves from the restrictions of corporate cost accounting. The unbridled success, until recently, of these entrepreneurial firms is a tribute to the independence that can be generated by community and kinship organization.

Pittsfield, comparatively, is in a better position to restructure its economy than those towns with rigidly single-commodity histories. The industrial clusters of paper, chemicals, and plastics manufacturing have made up for some of the decline of General Electric's productive infrastructure. The plastics and chemical industries, in particular, made significant gains during the 1980s. The number of small plastics plants grew from 25, in the early 1980s, to 38 in the 1990s. The owners of these small firms, fiercely independent and traditionally secretive, organized to accept a state grant of $200,000 to form a managerial network that has a full-time office manager.

Still, the downward turn continues. In 1991, the moldmakers and molders showed a 4.6 percent drop from 1990 in employment, faring better than the 7.6 percent decline for the industrial sector,[1] but not to compensate for the significant decline of industry in the region. The 1992 merger between GE aerospace and Martin Marietta further endangers the 3,000 employees currently employed by the plant.

Tourism is still regarded as a savior for the Pittsfield region. Even as employment dropped in this sector by 18.8 percent between 1988 and 1991, the *Berkshire Report* regards this industry as the wave of the future. It points to the "bright spot" of the increase in personal services employment, specifically noting the opening of the Ranch Spa that has created 400 jobs in the region since 1989. The Massachusetts Museum of Contemporary Art (MOCA), opened in North Adams in the abandoned Sprague Electric Plant, is another opportunity for tourist growth. Backed by $36 million in public funds, it is another project hoping to attract tourists to the Berkshires. But again, this optimism is not backed up by economic statistics. These jobs cannot make up for the substantial layoffs and declines in basic industry.

American communities and popular American culture use "development" to signify an economic growth pattern that benefits all concerned. The question of development for whom, or at the expense of what, is rarely an issue, particularly in communities in chronic need of tax revenue and jobs. Questions may arise around the kind of development that takes place. Wealthier landowners may succeed in zoning industrial or residential growth away from their neighborhoods. But this success does not alter the overarching belief that economic development is inherently beneficial, leading to improved housing, education, health, welfare, and opportunity. With economic growth as a desired end, planners take the focus off the unequal distribution of income with the magical thinking that future growth will be better or more equally distributed.

In the 1980s, the Reagan administration dismantled direct assistance to poor, rural, and restructuring communities. The Department of Housing and Urban Development's Office of Neighborhood Development disappeared. So did the Comprehensive Employment and Training Act. Low-income housing subsidies were all but eliminated. Antipoverty programs, a response by the Johnson administration to the start of American economic decline, were abolished (see Pierce and Steinbach, 1987). These achievements by those who wield power were only the start of a trend that currently has seen the last vestiges of the social safety net, the welfare system, ravaged by a Democratic president.[2] Our public medical and education systems are in ruins. Unemployment insurance has been so emaciated that it does not begin to alleviate the damage caused by the time it now takes to find work, even at minimum wages. Even Social Security, which all Americans pay for directly, is in danger of self-destructing. Power is becoming increasingly consolidated, backed by the American government, regardless of whether Democrats or Republicans are in office.

What we are left with is what Anthony Giddens (1994) has called "manufactured uncertainty." Communities are left with damage control and repair, while even some major corporations, through new discussions of "corporate citizenship," have started to question how their destruction of the environment and the attacks on the standard of living will affect their profit margins.

What is to be done? The cost-accounting approach is now an American way of life, even when it doesn't particularly succeed in saving the company money. Its predominance is visible because it is applied to about 80 percent of the wage distribution, the vast majority of U.S. households. For those not laid off, Gordon (1995) tells us, "*real spendable hourly earnings had fallen back [in 1993] to below the levels they had reached in 1962*, more than thirty years earlier" (1995:4, italics in the original). But as he goes on to note, total compensation for top executives has continued to soar through the

1990s. Gordon argues that there is a "bureaucratic burden" that has put U.S. corporations at a disadvantage with those overseas. In 1993, for example, one-quarter of all national income received in the nonfarm sector went to supervisory and nonproduction personnel:

> How is it possible that so many people spend at least some of their time bossing others? The basic principal is simple. If a labor-management system relies on hierarchical principals for managing and supervising its front-line employees on the shop and office floors, then it needs more than just the front line supervisors who directly oversee these production and supervisory workers. Who keeps the supervisors honest? What guarantees that those supervisors won't be in cohoots with their charges? In such a hierarchy, you need supervisors to supervise the supervisors . . . and supervisors above them . . . and managers to watch the higher level supervisors . . . and higher level managers to watch the lower level supervisors . . . and higher-level managers to watch the lower-level managers. A pyramid takes shape in which every level of supervision from the bottom on up is essential to the operations of the entire enterprise.

The creation of these layered levels of bureaucracy in the United States is a product of the unchecked capitalistic markets that those on the left have pointed. These unchecked markets, creating the growth of universal commodization, and economic polarization to which Marx pointed[3], also generate distrust and suspicion among corporations and between managers—who see their own profits in danger of dwindling.

The difference in ideology and orientation among corporations and communities is bound to the resources and structural power available to construct consensus. It is not enough to state that prudent planning requires the support of city managers without the realization that the capital may not be available to support expansion. Community businesses may also, as happened in Pittsfield, be dealing with competitive disadvantages beyond their control. While as short-term solutions, the energy expended on generating tax revenues is productive, the larger problem remains in the distribution of capital and its consequences. It is worth restating Castell's (1980) observation that the current crisis in American communities is not only economic, but political and ideological:

> The economic crisis, which has developed as a consequence of structural conditions triggered by the process of capital accumulation, results from the contradictions that are an expression of social relationships of production, distribution and management. The policies that will be used to deal with the crisis will be deter-

mined by the political processes of American society. (Castells, 1980:138).

For the population of Pittsfield, a strong community has continually confronted, as far as it is possible, the structural changes within the corporation by adapting its resources to meet changing requirements. The current restructuring of multinationals, however, means that new directions are needed that are indeed outside of the community's immediate arena. Communities have no chance with multinationals—the resources are simply too differentiated. Attempts to deal with planning difficulties associated with restructuring necessarily lead to the production of chaos, and the further masking of the relationships of class and power that define the discourse.

What is good for multinationals is not necessarily good for the communities they occupy. What is a profitable strategy for General Electric in Pittsfield has not been good for Pittsfield. Longer-term solutions to the crisis created by restructuring need to be tied to the confrontations on their terms—multinationally as well as nationally. Local policy that defines solutions by what Safa (1981) calls "narrow protectionism"—the "Buy American" campaigns and the attempts to institute tariffs on foreign products—do not succeed in providing a basis to confront the issues at their root—the point of production. How much of the production of American automobiles is actually done in the United States? What does it mean to say that one should only buy American cars? Some communities, as Safa notes, have instead urged their governments to work toward minimum Internal Labor Organization standards in wages, working conditions, and free trade unions in less developed countries. Compliance would improve living conditions in Third World countries, while lessening the competitive disadvantage of workers in the older industrial nations. The possibility of this strategy's being freely adopted by competitive capitalist states, however, is minimal without the social reorganization that is necessary to changes the structures of power. Giddens argues that there must be a concern to repair *damaged solidarities*, the divisions created by "individualism," the self-seeking, profit-maximizing behavior of the marketplace. The repudiation of individualism, however, is not the same as a sudden demand for selflessness. As Giddens continues,

> In a world of high reflexivity, an individual must achieve a certain degree of autonomy of action as a condition of being able to survive and forge a life; but autonomy is not the same as egoism and moreover implies *reciprocity* and *interdependence*. The issue of reconstructing social solidarities should therefore note be seen as one of protecting social cohesion around the edges of an egoistic marketplace. It should be understood as one of reconciling auton-

omy and interdependence in the various spheres of social life, including the economic domain. (1994:13)

A real option is the organization of unions on an international basis that recognize the way that working nationals are pitted against each other and can challenge the global hegemony of corporate multinational structures.

More immediately, Gordon proposes that a sharp increase in the minimum wage would create an upward pressure on wages and create counterpressures against the expansion of corporate bureaucracy. He also recommends an easing in labor laws that would make it easier to form unions that could counter destructive corporate moves. Last, he urges investment in firms with less top-heavy management relations, provided through tax incentives or special investment banks (1995:24–25).

For Pittsfield, these recommendations are directly applicable to the direction of development efforts. The Berkshire County Commission urges efforts to attract capital from major outside banks and investment firms. Although they do urge the creation of capital and credit opportunities for new and expanding businesses, these initiatives are discussed in the same breath as the building of more roads and the expansion of tourism. "Native" views need to be listened to. Small businesses in the Berkshires have shown the greatest growth. The statistics on city planning show that the creation of jobs is primarily a result of the expansion of small businesses located near urban neighborhoods, rather than the intervention of large companies. The 1979 survey by the Federal Economic Development Administration, for example, showed that small firms (twenty thirds of all new jobs in the United States, as well as almost *all* new jobs in New England. As Birch (1979:8) writes, "It appears, that it is the smaller corporations, despite their higher failure rates, that are aggressively seeking out most new opportunities, while the larger ones are primarily redistributing their operations."

Ultimately, development processes have to be reoriented to focus on human needs. As Leacock sums, "To talk of development means to talk of bringing an end to the present system of profit-making with its ever present threat of war. It means talking about the desperate need for a peaceful and economically secure world in which people, not profits, are the central social value" (1981:311).

Notes

Introduction

1. See Shepard Forman, Ed., *Diagnosing America* (Ann Arbor: University of Michigan Press, 1994). While this work does not directly discuss the availability and distribution of resources in American society, it does successfully point to issues that warrant further discussion.

2. Ideology is here broadly defined, derived from Stuart Hall, who tells us that it is "a direct reference to the world of *ideas*," and "entails the proposition that ideas are not self-sufficient, that their roots lie elsewhere, that something central about ids will be revealed if we can discover the nature of determinacy which non-ideas exert over ideas" (Hall, 1977:10). To this definition I would add that ideology is *subtext*, where the real meaning of the presentation of event subsumes the real motivation behind the occurrence.

3. Community development corporations, in particular, are a direct response to contracting federal involvement in development. Their rise parallels the beginnings of stagnation in the American economy, and they were largely federally supported until they were dismantled by the Reagan administration. For a discussion of these corporations, see Pierce and Steinbach (1987).

Chapter 2. Community and Context

1. The following summary of evolution of the American city is based on David Gordon (1984).

2. "The urban population increased from just over 200,000 in 1790 to more than 6 million in 1860. More important, the urban share of total population *reversed* its decline during the colonial period. Relative urban popula-

tion rose from one-twentieth of the American population in 1790 to one fifth in 1860" (Gordon, 1984:26).

3. For a discussion of the role of water in the development of industry in Pittsfield, see Nash (1989).

4. While in smaller cities, apparently, the "the non-industrial classes saw no necessary contradiction between private enterprise and gain on the one hand, and decent, humane social relations between workers and employers on the other. In the largest cities, it appears, relationships among the several classes were different. Workers were, in the transitional years, at least, no less likely to strike than workers in smaller cities. But the various strata of the middle class were much more hostile to the workers than their peers in smaller cities. Newspapers, politicians, and the middle classes usually opposed workers on strike. Facing such hostility, workers found it more difficult to fight their employers" (Gutman, 1963:48, quoted in Gordon, 1984:33).

Chapter 3. Restructuring

1. U.S. Bureau of Labor Statistics, Office of Productivity and Technology, "Output per Hour, Hourly Compensation, and Unit Labor Costs in Manufacturing, Twelve Economies, 1950–1993," unpublished tables, February 1995, table 13. Quoted in Gordon, 1996:258.

2. Gordon (1996:11) based on continuous Louis Harris Poll results.

3. "The private tailor is replaced by the ready-made clothes industry, the cobbler by the repair division of big department stores, shoe shops and factories, the cook by the mass production of pre-cooked meals in self-service restaurants . . . the housemaid or charwoman by the mechanization of these functions, in the shape of the vacuum cleaner, washing machines, dishwasher, and so on" (Mandel, 1972:386).

4. It should be noted that the rationalization process does encounter resistance and can be counterproductive. "It appears that the leading national economy at the time of the overall downturn is the most resistant at being penetrated by the downturn and hence engages in less merger activity. . . . [T]he general merger movement that brought about multinational enterprises administered through managerial hierarchies in the United States at the end of the nineteenth century acted more to reaffirm the traditional family form in Britain, It appears that their hegemonic position in world production impeded their structural reorganization necessary to emerge strengthened on the other side of the nineteenth century downturn" (Mandel, 1972: 32).

5. "If the present downturn generates a wave of mergers, the result for the United States will be to reaffirm the 'traditional' private multinational rather than move on to the state owned firm. Chrysler provides a good example. The government 'bail out' of Chrysler allows it to continue in a world auto market where it appears certain to fail. Rather than making Chrysler a state firm, possibly in combination with other auto manufacturers, the American solution is to prop up the private multinational, and as such preserve what may be an increasing outdated form of industrial enterprise—outdated in that the addition of the state will give the state owned enterprise certain competition advantages over the more traditional multinational—such as the ability of the state to absorb losses allowing the firm to continue without having to show immediate profits or fear immediate bankruptcy, and the obvious preferential access to state financing and hidden subsidies" (Bergensen, 1982:37).

A direct example of this kind of competition between private enterprises and state owned firms can be found in Pittsfield through the analysis of the plastics industry, discussed in chapter 5.

6. For a discussion of the role of research and development in the dissemination of new technology, see David Noble, *America by Design.*

7. A full discussion of the mall is included in chapter 4.

8. Coming from an "open class system" (as the sociologists call it) where status is achieved rather than inherited or automatic and both privilege and authority have to be "deserved" or "justified" or "won" (by merit, not force), Americans have woven effort, achievement, and success through and through the fabric of their culture and their lives. Activist, pragmatic, moralizing values (rather than say, contemplative, theorizing, rhetorical, or sensual, ascetic, or mystical ones) are interconnected and integrated in the American character. "Success" in "serious effort" is both a personal goal, an ethical imperative, and the mark of a man (or a woman).

Chapter 4. The Region and Industry in History

1. "The willingness of millowners and managers to cooperate so fully with one another undoubtably stemmed from the fact that the textile firms in this period were owned and directed by a narrow circle of capitalists known as the Boston Associates. . . . The bonds of common interests among the stockholders and directors led to a sharing of technology, resources and information that was remarkable. Companies routinely shared architectural drawings, wage lists, figures on cost of production, even prices of equipment and extra cotton stock. . . . One Nashua, New Hampsire agent cautioned against a proposed wage cut by noting, 'for us to think of reducing wages

before they do at Lowell would in my opinion be bad policy.' . . . Taken together, the evidence provides assurance that in examining the experience of women workers in the Lowell mills we are also addressing broader trends and issues relevant to working women in other factory towns of New England during this period" (Dublin, 1979:11).

2. Hareven and Langenbach note that the Amoskeag workers experienced a close integration between the family and the factory. "Husbands and wives, or brothers and sisters, often toiled in similar or related occupations. Most important, except for the mechanical departments for the dye houses, workrooms were not segregated by sex. Hence, members of the same family often worked together, carrying their friendships and family ties with them. It is therefore not surprising that many of the workers viewed the factory 'like a family' " (1978:118).

3. As Gutman tells us, "Even though American society itself underwent radical structural changes between 1815 and the First World War, the shifting composition of its wage-earning population meant that traditional customs, rituals, and beliefs repeatedly helped shape the behavior of its diverse working class groups. The street battle in 1843 that followed Irish efforts to prevent New York City authorities from stopping pigs from running loose in the streets is but one example of the force of old styles of behavior" (Gutman, 1977:63).

4. This is true in present-day Pittsfield as it was then in New Hampshire. There is a tendency to refer to the corporation as *the GE.*

5. In general, the physical arrangements of home and work were arranged by the company to maximize control: "Workers were isolated from the larger world while on the job; outside influences were not allowed to 'intrude' and disturb the work. The arrangement of buildings thus reinforced the control that machine technology and an inflexible work force timetable gave managment over the work process and the worker" (Dublin, 1979:61), and "Housing for female workers kept wage levels down, but there was also an instrument of social control. For women boarding houses were part of a broader version of corporate paternalism. . . . Twice in the 1830's, however, mill managment took a course of action that led women workers to rebel. In February 1834 and October 1836, women workers struck to oppose first reductions in wages and then increases in the board rates charged in company housing" (Ibid., 77–78).

6. The availability of male immigrants as cheap labor, particularly those from Ireland who had the experience of the famine behind them, blurred the traditional line beteween male and female labor: With the entry of male immigrants at wage levels considerably below those of native-born

men, the wages of the lowest paid men and the highest paid women over-lapped for the first time" (Dublin, 1979:142).

7. "There is only one remedy, and that is government control of the means of production and transportation" (William B. Adams, a carpenter from West Quincy, quoted in Keyssar, 1987:237).

8. Keyssar (1986) notes that the connotation of "unemployed" in the late nineteenth century took on moral overtones, and labor leaders therefore urged the use of the term "disemployed": "We have used the term dis-employed as more expressive and true . . . than the ordinary, and more gen-eral term un-employed—which includes not only this class but all who are voluntarily or involuntarily without employment; the sick and the incompe-tent, the thriftless, the lazy and vicious, the willing paupers and the profes-sional beggars—all belong to the comprehensive and motley crowd of the un-employed; and we protest against the injustice of associating-even in idea—the honest, industrious workers—who are idle from no fault of their own—with the same motley crowd" (1877: *The Vindicator*, quoted in Keyssar, 1987:3).

9. According to the figures compiled from Dun and Bradstreet's Business Economics Division, business closings through failure have been higher in New England than in the South Central Region, the South Atlantic Region, and the South Central Region in every year since 1955 (Harrison, 1982:35).

10. Metzgar (1980) has argued that the red baiting and union challeng-ing of the 1950s led to a period of accession by unions in exchange for the institutionalization of benefits through the collective bargaining system. Harrison (1982:47) comments that this "social contract" was to last a quarter of a century before it was challenged by management in the 1970s.

11. See Harrison (1981). .

12. He goes on to summarize that "we find that few of those who leave the generally declining, older mill-based industries of the region are able to move into the relatively good jobs in growth sectors such as high-tech (or even into the still higher-paying jobs in the older, established capital goods industries such as aircraft). Relatively few of the mill workers move away from the region. But whether they move or not, they tend not to be hired by high-tech companies. The lesson seems clear: The region simply does not hold enough new, well-paying jobs in the growth industries to absorb those displaced by industrial disinvestment, and the jobs created in sectors such as high-tech are in any case going to other people, including many recruited from outside the region altogether" (Harrison 1981:95).

Chapter 5. The Pittsfield Community

1. For a complete discussion of early industry in Pittsfield and the reliance on water power and rights, see Nash (1989).

2. "The Pittsfield Woolen Company updated its buildings and machinery after a fire in 1861. The owners were in a position to buy out the Bel Aire Manufacturing Company and replace their old building and machinery with new more sophisticated cards and looms. There were few women and girls employed in the new mills with only one-quarter to one-fifth of the workforce of about 150 being female. This seems to have been a response to the technical innovations that were deskilling the work process and reducing the jobs that women had held. New woolen companies were formed, with the C. Russell Manufacturing Company in 1886 and W. E. Tillotson Manufacturing Company in 1889 coming into being at a time when these older companies were in decline. Their workforce of 800 to 900 workers was twice the numbers employed in earlier mills. The A. H. Rice Company began production of silk braid in 1887 using new complex machinery to turn out specialty products. Machine shops owned by William Clark and Company came under the ownership of E. D. Jones who later became a producer of manufacturing machinery, some of which was sold to Crane's expanding industry. This company attracted a core of metal workers that expanded the skilled labor force" (Nash, 1989).

3. Davis (1986) has argued that the difference between communities like Lynn (and by association, Pittsfield) and Fall River was the ability to forge a working-class culture and working-class institutions outside of the workplace. He attributes this difference to the ways in which immigrants were incorporated into the community, largely dependent on the numbers of immigrants arriving at once. He furthermore concludes that "Unfortunately, most of industrial America was more like Fall River than Lynn. Whereas the Western European class struggles of the 1880s and 1890s had spun a web of integrating proletarian institutions (ranging from workmen's clubs, cooperatives, and 'labor churches' to *casas del pueblo* and workers' educational societies), the U.S. labor movement of the late nineteenth century, as we have seen, failed to generate a working class 'culture' that could overcome ethno-religious alignments outside the workplace" (Davis, 1986:41).

4. Government spending figured high in the development of the entire region after World War II. Harrison states that "Government orders directly stimulated production in other industries that were either already important in the region (such as textiles in Nashua, New Hampshire, and shipbuilding in Bat, Maine, Quincy, Massachusetts, and New London, Connecticut) or which would soon become so. . . . The development of the

(at first electromechanical, later electronic) computer industry grew out of the wartime military demand for precise calculations of shell trajectories and in connection with the Manhattan Project that produced the first atom bomb" (1982:27).

5. Defense spending in Massachusetts in 1986 equaled $1,500 for every citizen in the state. GE Pittsfield received its share for high-technology missile system development and the transmission for the Bradley Fighting Vehicle. The infusion of these monies softened the blow of the closing down of the power transformer division, when many of those laid-off workers who had seniority were transferred to ordnance.

6. It is important to note that as a trend, unemployed workers do not have the capital or the tools to increase domestic labor. Paul and Wallace (1985:223) note that households cannot really achieve independence from market services. They put forward a "polarization thesis," which suggests "the overwhelming dependence on all forms of informal work, including self provisioning, on the money from formal employment" (1985:224). They note, however, that the level of cooperation is dependent on culturally derived values.

Chapter 6. Development Strategies

1. They state, for example, that "urban governments are organized in ways which allow them to absorb political discontent through political participation which is limited to agencies and issues which do not impinge upon economic growth" (Friedland, Piven, and Alford, 1984:279). This separation can be seen in a concrete sense in Pittsfield by the many public forums available to citizens to discuss community issues, while the issues of "tax vacations" and other concessions to the corporation are not subject to public scrutiny.

2. The view that the elites are obstacles to development is, perhaps not surprisingly, similar to the modernization theorists who advocated widespread entrepreneurship for the purposes of development.

3. Two years later the city was to blame for the lack of progress on downtown development, The Fisher Group complaining that "as of this moment, we're quite frustrated as to how this is going to happen . . . we try to be understanding" (*Berkshire Eagle*, July 15, 1983).

4. For an interesting discussion of the transformation of American society by the automobile industry, and the restructuring of corporate capital that this entailed, see Edsforth (1987).

Chapter 8. Economic Development and Social Responsibility

1. It is interesting to note that as with all cost accounting principles, the salient feature is obtaining the lowest possible cost rather than regulating profit.

2. This reaction by the corporation followed the banning of PCBs in Japan, after workers who had eaten contaminated rice became ill.

3. Nelson (n.d.), "PCBs: An Industry Problem?"

Epilogue

1. Berskhire County Community Profile, Massachusetts Department of Housing and Community Development (1995:5).

2. In 1994, 51% of Pittsfield's registered voters were Democrat; 13% were Republican. The difference reflects the perceived orientation of these political parties. What is more interesting, given current political conditions, is that 36% of registered voters were unenrolled in a party.

3. For a discussion of this phenomena, see Giddons (1994).

Bibliography

Aglietta, M. 1979. *A Theory of Capitalist Regulation: The U.S. Experience.* London: New Left Publishers.

Alonso, W. 1965. "Location Theory." In J. Friedman and W. Alonso (eds.), *Economic Development and Planning.* Cambridge, Mass.: MIT Press.

Anderson, P. 1968. "Components of the National Culture." *New Left Review* 50.

Anderson, P. 1976. *Considerations on Western Marxism.* London: New Left Books.

Anderson, P. 1984. *In the Tracks of Historical Materialism.* Chicago: University of Chicago Press.

Anthony, P. D. 1977. *The Ideology of Work.* London: Tavistock.

Appadurai, A. 1986. *The Social Life of Things.* New York: Cambridge University Press.

Applebawm, H. 1986. *Work: A Reader.* Albany: State University of New York Press.

Arensberg, A. 1961. "The Community as Object and as Sample." *American Anthropologist* 63.

Arensberg, A. n.d. "Assumptions of American Culture." Washington, D.C.: Foreign Service Institute, U.S. Department of State.

Asad, T. 1970. *Anthropology and the Colonial Encounter.* Cambridge: Cambridge University Press.

Asad, T. 1979. "Anthropology and the Analysis of Ideology." *Man* 14(4).

Austin, D. J. 1979. "History and Symbols in Ideology: A Jamaican Example." *Man* 14.

Bagbh, P. H. 1953. "Culture and the Causes of Culture." *American Anthropologist* 55.

Balachandran, M. 1976. *Malls and Shopping Centers: A Selected Bibliography.* Monticello, Ill.: Council of Planning Libraries.

Balfuch, P. and J. M. Limbor. 1968. "Changes in the Industrial Distribution of the World Labor Force by Region, 1880-1960." *International Labor Review* 98(4): 311-336.

Bally, R. 1980. "On the Holism of a World-Systems Perspective." In T. Hopkins and I. Wallerstein (eds.), *Processes of the World System*. Beverly Hills, Calif.: Sage.

Banton, M. (ed.). 1966. *The Social Anthropology of Complex Societies*. ASA Monographs 4. London: Tavistock.

Bender, T. 1978. *Community and Social Change in America*. Baltimore: Johns Hopkins University Press.

Bergensen, A. 1982. "Economic Crisis and Merger Movements: 1880's Britian and 1980's United States." In E. Friedman (ed.), *Ascent and Decline in the World System*. Beverly Hills, Calif.: Sage.

Berger, B. 1968. "Myths of American Suburbia." In R. E. Paul (ed.), *Readings in Urban Sociology*. Oxford: Pergamon.

Bergquist, C. (ed.), 1984. *Labor in the Capitalist World Economy*. Beverly Hills, Calif.: Sage.

Berkshire County Development Commission. 1981. *Berkshire County Manufacturer's Directory*.

Berry, B. 1961. "City Size Distributions and Economic Development." *Economic Development and Cultural Change* 9(4): 573-88.

Berry, B. 1965. "Cities as Systems within Systems of Cities." In J. Friedman and W. Alonso (eds.), *Regional Development and Planning*. Cambridge, Mass.: MIT Press.

Berry, B. 1971. "City Size and Economic Development." In L. Jakobson and V. Prakash (eds.), *Urbanization and National Development*. Beverly Hills, Calif.: Sage.

Birch, D. L. 1979. "The Job Generation Process." Cambridge, Mass.: MIT Program on Neighborhood and Regional Change.

Birch, D. L. 1987. *Job Creation in America: How the Smallest Companies Put the Most People to Work*. New York: Free Press.

Blackaby, F. (ed.) 1979. *Deindustrialization*. London: Heinemann Educational Books.

Blatzell, E. D. 1979. *Puritan Boston and Quaker Philadelphia*. Boston: Beacon Press.

Blicksilver, J. 1979. "Kinship and Friendship in the Emergence of a Family-Controlled Southern Enterprise: Life Insurance Company of Georgia: 1891-1950." In S. Greenfield, A. Strickon, and R. Aubrey. (eds.), *Entrepreneurs in Cultural Context*. Albuquerque: University of New Mexico Press.

Bluestone, B. 1972. "Economic Crisis and the Law of Uneven Development." *Politics and Society* 2(4).

Bluestone, B. and B. Harrison. 1982. *The Deindustrialization of America.* New York: Basic Books.

Bodnar, J. 1978. "Immigration and Modernization: The Case of Slavic Peasants in Industrial America." *Journal of Social History.*

Borloy, H. 1979. "Social Control Theories of Urban Politics." *Social Science Quarterly* 59(4): 605-21.

Bornschier, V. 1981. "Dependent Industrialization in the World Economy." *Journal of Conflict Resolution* 25:3.

Boulding, K. 1978. "The City as Element in the International System." In L. S. Bourne and J. W. Simmons (eds.), *Systems of Cities.* New York: Oxford University Press.

Bourdieu, P. 1977. *Outline of a Theory of Practice.* Cambridge: Cambridge University Press.

Bourdieu, P. 1984. *Distinction: A Social Critique of the Judgement of Taste.* Cambridge: Cambridge University Press.

Boyte, H. C. and S. M. Evans. 1984. "Strategies in Search of America: Cultural Radicalism, Populism and Democratic Culture." *Socialist Review* 75-76: 73-102.

Braverman, H. 1974. *Labor and Monopoly Capital.* New York: Monthly Review.

Brecher, J. 1979. "Roots of Power: Employees and Workers in the Electrical Products Industry." In R. Zimbalist (ed.), *Case Studies in the Labor Process.* New York: Monthly Review.

Brecher, J. 1982. *Strike.* Boston: South End Press.

Brody, D. 1979. "The Old Labor and the New: In Search of an American Working Class." *Labor History* 20.

Brook, E. and D. Finn 1980. "Working Class Images of Society and Community Studies." In *On Ideology.* London: Hutchinson.

Bruchey, S. 1968. *The Roots of American Economic Growth 1607-1861.* New York: Harper & Row.

Bryden, T. 1973. *Tourism and Development: A Case Study of the Commonwealth Caribbean.* London: Cambridge University Press.

Burawoy, M. 1973. "The Functions and Reproduction of Migrant Labor: Comparative Material From Southern Africa and the United States." *American Journal of Sociology.*

Burawoy, M. 1979. *Manufacturing Consent.* Chicago: University of Chicago Press.

Burawoy, M. 1983. *The Politics of Production.* London: Verso.

Calahan, R. and S. Watson. 1984. *A Strategy for Economic Development in Berkshire County.* Cambridge, Mass.: John F. Kennedy School of Government, Harvard University.

Cardoso, F. H. 1973. "Associated-Dependent Development: Theoretical and Practical Implications." In A. Stephan (ed.). *Authoritarian Brazil.* New Haven, Conn.: Yale University Press.

Castells. M. 1980. *The Economic Crisis and American Society.* Princeton, N.J.: Princeton University Press.

Chase-Dunn, C. 1979. "Comparative Research on World Systems Characteristics." *Industrial Studies Quarterly* 23(4): 601–23.

Chase-Dunn, C. 1983. "Urbanization in the World System: New Directions for Research." *Comparative Urban Growth* 9(2):41–46.

Cohen, A. 1969. "Political Anthropology: The Analysis of the Symbolism of Power Relations." *Man.*

Comoroff, J. 1987. *Body of Power, Spirit of Resistance.* Chicago: University of Chicago Press.

Cottrell, W. F. 1951, "Death by Dieselization: A Case Study in the Reaction to Technological Change." *American Sociological Review* 16: 359–65.

Coward, R. and J. Ellis. 1977. *Language and Materialism: Developments in Semiology and the Theory of the Subject.* London: Routledge and Kegan Paul.

Cumbler, J. T. 1979. *Working Class Community in Industrial America: Work, Leisure and Struggle in Two Industrial Cities, 1880-1930.* Westport, Conn.: Greenwood Press.

Davis, K. 1955. "The Origin and Growth of Urbanization in the World." *American Journal of Sociology* 60: 429–37.

Davis, M. 1980. "Labour in American Politics." *New Left Review* 123.

Davis, M. 1986. *Prisoners of the American Dream.* London: Verso.

deKadt, E. 1976. "Tourism, Passport to Development?" In *Perspectives in the Social and Cultural Effects of Tourism in Developing Countries.* Washington, D.C.

Dennis, N. 1956. *Coal Is Our Life.* London: Tavistock

Dore, R. 1973. *British Factory-Japanese Factory.* Berkeley: University of California Press.

Dowd, D. 1956. "A Comparative Analysis of Economic Development in the American South and West." *Journal of Economic History* 16.

"Downsized, but Not Out: A Mill Town's Tale." *New York Times*, March 9, 1997.

Drennan, M. 1983. "Local Economy and Local Revenues." In M. Hanton and C. Brecher (eds.), *Setting Municipal Priorities, 1984.* New York: New York University Press.

Dublin, T. 1979. *Women at Work.* New York: Columbia University Press.

Dubois, C. 1955. "The Dominant Value Profile of American Culture." *American Anthropologist* 57: 1232–39.

Dumhoff, G. William. 1974. *The Bohemian Grove*. New York: Harper & Row.

Eddy, E. 1987. *Applied Anthropology in America*. New York: Columbia University Press.

Eddy, E. and W. L. Partridge (eds.). 1987. *Applied Anthropology in America*. New York: Columbia University Press.

Edel, M. 1983. "Capitalism, Accumulation and the Explanation of Urban Phenomena." In M. Dear and A. Scott (eds.), *Urbanization and Urban Planning in Capitalist Society*. New York: Methuen.

Edsforth, R. 1987. *Class Conflict and Cultural Consensus: The Making of a Mass Consumer Society in Flint, Michigan*. New Brunswick, N.J.: Rutgers University Press.

Eisenmenger, R. 1967. *The Dynamics of Growth in New England's Economy, 1870-1964*. Middletown, Conn.: Wesleyan University Press.

Erikson, K. 1976. *Everything in Its Path*. New York: Simon & Schuster.

Faler, P. G. 1981. *Mechanics and Manufacturing in the Early Industrial Revolution: Lynn, Massachussets, 1780-1860*. Boston: Beacon Press.

"Fed Survey Says Higher Pay Mostly Eludes Workers." *New York Times*, March 13, 1997.

Folson, M. S. and S. Lebar (eds.). 1980. *The Philosophy of Manufacturers: The Early Debates over Industrialization in the United States*. Vol. 1. Cambridge, Mass.: MIT Press.

Form, W. 1985. *Divided We Stand: Working Class Stratification in America*. Urbana: University of Illinois Press.

Forman, S. 1994. *Diagnosing America: Anthropology and Public Engagement*. Ann Arbor: University of Michigan Press.

Friedland, R., F. F. Piven, and R. R. Alford. 1984. "Political Conflict, Urban Structure and the Fiscal Crisis." In W. K. Tabb and L. Sawers (eds.), *Marxism and the Metropolis*. New York: Oxford University Press.

Friedmann, J. 1987. *Planning in the Public Domain*. Princeton, N.J.: Princeton University Press.

Gamst, F. C. 1977. "An Integrating View of the Underlying Premises of an Industrial Ethnology in the United States and Canada." *Anthropological Quarterly* 50(1).

Gans, H. J. 1969. *The Urban Villagers: Group and Class in the Life of Italian Americans*. New York: Free Press.

Garn, H. A. and L. L. Ledebur. 1981. *The Estimation of Development Impacts*. Washington, D.C.: The Urban Institute Press.

"G.E. Chief's Total '96 Pay: $30 Million." *New York Times*, March 3, 1997.

Gellner, E. 1974. *Legitimation of Belief.* Cambridge: Cambridge University Press.

Gellner, E. 1978. "Notes towards a Theory of Ideology." *L'Homme* 18.

Gershuny, J. I. and I. D. Miles. 1983. *The New Service Economy: The Transformation of Employment in Industrial Societies.* London: Frances Pinter.

Giddens, A. 1994. Beyond Left and Right. Stanford, Calif.: Stanford University Press.

Ginzberg, E. amd G. J. Vogta. 1981. "The Service Sector in the U.S. Economy." *Scientific American* 244(3): 48–55.

Godelier, M. 1980. "Work and Its Representations: A Research Proposal." *History Workshop Journal* 10.

Godfrey, M. 1986. *Global Unemployment: The New Challenge to Economic Theory.* New York: St. Martin's.

Goldthorpe, J. H. 1964. "Social Stratification in Industrial Society." *Sociological Review Monograph* 8.

Goodman, R. 1980. *The Last Entrepreneurs.* New York: Simon & Schuster.

Gordon, D. M. 1979. "The Working Poor: Towards a State Agenda." Washington, D.C.: Council of State Planning Agencies.

Gordon, D. M. 1984. "Capitalist Development and the History of American Cities." In W. K. Tabb and L. Sawers (eds.), *Marxism and the Metropolis.* New York: Oxford University Press.

Gordon, D. M. 1995. "Underpaid Workers, Bloated Corporations: Two Pieces in the Puzzle of U.S. Economic Decline." Paper presented on the occasion of the inauguration of the Dorothy H. Hirshon Professorship of Economics, New School for Social Research.

Gordon, D. M. 1996. *Fat and Mean.* New York: Martin Kessler Books.

Gordon, D. M., R. Edwards, and M. Reich. 1982. *Segmented Work, Divided Workers: The Historical Transformation of Labor in the United States.* New York: Cambridge University Press.

Gorz, A. 1984. *Farewell to the Working Class: An Essay on Post-Industrial Socialism.* Boston: South End Press.

Greenberg, B. 1985. *Worker and Community Response to Industrialization in a Nineteenth Century City: Albany, New York, 1850–1884.* Albany: State University of New York Press.

Greenfield, S. M., A. Stricken. and R. Aubrey (eds.). 1979. *Entrepreneurs in Cultural Context.* Albuquerque: University of New Mexico Press.

Greenwood, D. S. 1972. "Tourism as an Aspect of Change: A Spanish Basque Case." *Ethnology* 11: 80–91.

Gullin, J. 1955. "National and Regional Culture Values in the United States." *Social Forces* 34: 107–13.

Gutman, H. 1966. *Work, Culture and Society in Industrializing America.* New York: Vintage.

Gutman, H. G. and D. H. Bell. 1987. *The New England Working Class and the New Labor History.* Urbana: University of Illinois Press.

Hagen, E. 1962. *On the Theory of Social Change.* Homewood: Dorsey Press.

Hall, S. 1984. "The Hinterland of Science: Ideology and the 'Sociology of Knowledge'." Working Papers in Culture Studies no. 10, London: School of Economics.

Hammond, B. 1957. "The Individual in an Industrial Civilization." In F. Keesing, B. J. Siegel, and B. Hammond (eds.), *Social Anthropology and Industry: Some Exploratory Workpapers.* Palo Alto, Calif.: Department of Anthropology, Stanford University.

Hannerz, U. 1969. *Soulside: Inquiriers into Ghetto Culture and Community.* New York: Columbia University Press.

Hannerz, U. 1980. *Exploring the City.* New York: Columbia University Press.

Harding, C. F. III. 1955. "The Social Anthropology of American Industry." *American Anthropologist* 57.

Hareven, T. K. 1975. "Family Time and Industrial Time: Family and Work in a Planned Corporation Town." *Journal of Urban History* (May).

Hareven, T. K. and R. Langenbach. 1978. *Amoskeag.* New York: Pantheon.

Harrison, B. 1981. *The New England Economy Project: Case Study Summaries, Policy Analysis and Research Methodology.* Report prepared for the Office of Economic Analysis and Research, Economic Development Administration, U.S. Department of Commerce. Washington, D.C.: U.S. Department of Commerce.

Harrison, B. 1982. "Rationalization, Restructuring and Industrial Reorganization in Older Regions: The Economic Transformation of New England Since World War II." *Working Paper* no. 72. Boston: Joint Center for Urban Studies of MIT and Harvard University.

Harvey, D. 1982. *The Limits of Capital.* Chicago: University of Chicago Press.

Harvey, D. 1985. *The Urbanization of Capital: Studies in the History and Theory of Urbanization.* Baltimore: Johns Hopkins University Press.

Heller, A. 1974. *The Theory of Need in Marx.* London: Billing and Sons.

Helm J. (ed.). 1986. *Social Contexts in American Ethnography.* Proceedings of the American Ethnological Society. Washington, D.C.: American Anthropological Association.

Henretta, J. A. 1977. "The Study of Social Mobility: Ideological Assumptions and Conceptual Bias." *Labor History* (Spring).

Henry, J. 1966. "A Theory for an Anthropological Analysis of American Culture." *Anthropological Quarterly* 39.

Herman, A. 1997. *The Idea of Decline in Western History*. New York: Free Press.

Hill, J. H. 1985. "The Grammar of Consciousness and the Consciousness of Grammar." *American Ethnologist* 12(4).

Hingham, J. (ed.). 1979. *Ethnic Leadership in America*. Baltimore: Johns Hopkins University Press.

Hobsbawm, E. 1972. "Class Consciousness in History." In I. Meszaros (ed.), *Aspects of History and Class Consciousness*. London: Herder and Herder.

Hoggart, R. 1957. *The Uses of Literacy*. London: Penguin.

Hollisteiner, M. and M. E. Lopez. 1976. "City Size Effects, Trends, and Policies." *Science* 193: 856–63.

Howell, Joseph T. 1973. *Hard Living on Clay Street*. Garden City, N.Y.: Anchor/Doubleday.

Huaco, E. A. 1986. "Ideology and General Theory: The Case of Sociological Functionalism." *Comparative Studies in Society and History* 28(1).

Humberger, E. 1981. "The Enterprise Zone Fallacy." *Journal of Community Action*, September-October.

Humphries, J. 1977. "The Working Class Family, Women's Liberation and Class Struggle: The Case of Nineteenth Century British History." *Review of Radical Political Economics* 9(3).

Innes, S. 1983. *Labor in a New Land: Economy and Society in Seventeenth Century Springfield*. Princeton, N.J.: Princeton University Press.

Jacobs, J. 1969. *The Economy of Cities*. New York: Random House.

Jelavich, M. S. 1984. "Economic Impact of Potential New Industries in a Four State Area." *American Economic Review* 74(1).

Jensen, M. 1965. *Regionalism in America*. Madison: University of Wisconsin Press.

Johnson, D. L. 1983. "Class Analysis and Dependency." in R. H. Chilcote and D. L. Johnson (eds.), *Theories of Development: Mode of Production or Dependency*. Beverly Hills, Calif.: Sage.

Jones, T. F. 1987. *Entrepreneurism: The Mythical, the True and the New*. New York: Donald Fire.

Kessing, F. M. B. J. Siegel, and B. Hammond. 1957. *Social Anthropology and Industry: Some Exploratory Workpapers*. Palo Alto, Calif.: Department of Anthropology, Stanford University.

Keyssar, A. 1987. "Unemployment and the Labor Movement in Massachusetts, 1870–1916." In H. Gutman and D. H. Bell (eds.), *The New England Working Class and the New Labor History*. Urbana: University of Illinois Press.

Keyssar, A. 1988. *Out of Work: The First Century of Unemployment in Massachusetts*. New York: Cambridge University Press.

Kimball, S. T. 1955. "Problems of Studying American Culture." *American Anthropologist* 57.

Kitching, G. 1985. "The Meaning of Development." In his *Development and Underdevelopment in Historical Perspective*. New York: Methuen.

Komarovsky, M. 1971. *The Unemployed Man and His Family*. New York: Octagon Books.

Kowinski, W. S. 1985. *The Malling of America: An Inside Look at the Great Consumer Paradise*. New York: William Morrow.

Lamb, R. K. 1952. "The Entrepreneur and the Community." In W. Miller (ed.), *Men in Business*. London: Cambridge University Press.

Leach, W. R. 1984. "Transformations in a Culture of Consumption: Women and Department Stores, 1890-1925." *Journal of American History* 71: 278-85.

LeClau, E. 1977. *Politics and Ideology in Marxist Theory*. London: New Left Books.

Leacock, E. 1984. *Myths of Male Dominance*. New York: Monthly Review.

Leacock, E. 1985. "Individuals and Society in Anthropological Theory." *Dialectical Anthropology* 10.

Leacock, E. and H. K. Safa. 1986. *Women's Work*. South Hadley, Mass.: Bergin and Garvey.

Leeds, A. 1973. "Locality Power in Relation to Supralocal Power Institutions." in A. Southall (ed.), *Urban Anthropology*. London: Tavistock.

Lesser, A. 1961. "Social Fields and the Evolution of Society." *Southwestern Journal of Anthropology* 17.

Levitt, T. 1976. "The Industrialization of Service." *Harvard Business Review* 54 (September): 63-74.

Lewis, W. D. 1984. "The State of Development Theory." *American Economic Review* 74(1).

Licht, W. 1984. "Divisions of Labor History." *Reviews in American History* 473-502.

Lichtheim, G. 1967. *The Concept of Ideology and Other Essays*. New York: Vintage.

Liebow, Elliot. 1967. *Tally's Corner: A Study of Negro Street Corner Men*. Boston: Little, Brown.

Lindberg, L. N., R. Alford, C. Crouch, and C. Offe (eds.). *Stress and Contradiction in Modern Capitalism: Public Policy and the Theory of the State*. Lexington, Mass.: D. C. Heath and Company.

Lipsitz, G. 1982. *Class and Culture in Cold War America*. South Hadley, Mass.: Bergin and Garvey.

Lockwood, D. 1975. "Sources of Variation in Working Class Images of Society." In C. Bulmer (ed.), *Working Class Images of Society.* London: Routledge and Kegan Paul.

Losch, A. 1965. "The Nature of Economic Regions." In J. Friedman and W. Alonso (eds.), *Economic Development and Planning.* Cambridge, Mass.: MIT Press.

Lotta, R. 1984. *America in Decline.* Vol. 1. Chicago: Banner Press.

Lyford, J. 1966. *The Airtight Cage: A Study of New York's West Side.* New York: Harper& Row.

MacCabe,C. 1979. "On Discourse." *Economy and Society* 8(2).

MacFarlane, A. 1978. *The Origins of English Individualism.* New York: Basil Blackwell.

Macfarlane, A. 1987. *The Culture of Capitalism.* New York: Basil Blackwell.

Machlup, F. 1962. *The Production and Distribution of Knowledge in the United States.* Princeton, N.J.: Princeton University Press.

MacKenzie, D. 1984. "Marx and the Machine." *Technology and Culture* 25.

Mandel, E. 1972. *Late Capitalism.* London: New Left Books.

Mandel, E. 1975. *The Second Slump.* London: New Left Books.

Mandel, E. 1992. *Power and Money.* New York: Verso.

Markusen, A. 1985. *Profit Cycles, Oligopoly and Regional Development.* Cambridge, Mass.: MIT Press.

Massachusetts Department of Housing and Community Development. 1995. *Community Profiles: Berkshire County.* Boston, Jane W. Gumble, Director.

Massachusetts Department of Commerce. 1983. *Massachusetts Business Incentives.*

Massachusetts Department of Commerce and Development. 1982. *All the Facts on Incentives for Business in Massachussetts.*

Massachusetts Department of Commerce. n.d. *Massachusetts—Creating the Future.*

Massachusetts Division of Employment Security. 1979. *Massachusetts Job Market Indicators 1972-1978.*

Massachusetts Division of Employment Security. 1980. *Paper Allied Products Industry in Massachusetts.*

Massachusetts Division of Employment Security. 1982a. *Annual Planning Information Report, Pittsfield LMA.*

Massachusetts Division of Employment Security. 1982b. *Employment and Wages in Massachusetts. SMSA's Labor Areas 1980-1982.*

Massachusetts Division of Employment Security. 1982c. *Employment and Wages, Cities and Towns 1980-1982.*

Massachusetts Division of Employment Security. 1983. *Compendium of Massachusetts Labor Market Trends 1970-1981.*

Massachusetts Division of Employment Security. 1984a. *Annual Planning Information Report, Fiscal Year 1983: Western Massachusetts.*

Massachusetts Division of Employment Security. 1984b. *Associated SDA's 1984.*

Massachusetts Division of Employment Security. 1984c. *Industry and Occupational Analysis.*

Massachusetts Division of Employment Security. 1984d. *Labor Market Information for Affirmative Action Programs, 1983.*

Massachusetts Division of Employment Security. 1985. *Compendium of Massachusetts Labor Market Trends 1970-1983.*

McKelvey, B. 1963. *The Urbanization of America, 1860-1915.* New Brunswick, N.J.: Rutgers University Press.

McNetting, R., R. R. Wilk, and E. J. Arnould (eds.). 1976 *Comparative and Historical Studies of the Domestic Group.* Berkeley: University of California Press.

Mead, M. 1942. *And Keep Your Powder Dry: An Anthropologist Looks at America.* New York: William Morrow.

Merry, S. E. 1986. "Everyday Understanding of the Law in Working Class America." *American Ethnologist* 13(2).

Meszaros, I. 1972. "Contingent and Necessary Class Consciousness." In I. Meszaros (ed.), *Aspects of History and Class Consciousness.* New York: Herder and Herder.

Miller, Z. L. 1973. *The Urbanization of Modern America: A Brief History.* New York: Harcourt.

Mingione, E. 1983. "Informalization, Restructuring and the Survival Strategies of the Working Class." *International Journal of Urban and Regional Research* 7(3).

Montgomery, D. 1978a. "Gutman's Nineteenth Century America." *Labor History* 19.

Montgomery, D. 1978b. "The Working Classes of the Pre-Industrial American City." *Labor History* 19.

Montgomery, D. 1979. *Worker's Control in America.* New York: Cambridge University Press.

Mullings, L. (ed.) 1987. Cities of the United States: Studies in Urban Anthropology. New York: Columbia University Press.

Nash, J. and M.-P. Fernandez Kelly (eds.). 1983. *Women, Men, and the International Division of Labor.* Albany: State University of New York Press.

Nash J. and M. Kirsch. 1987. "Corporate Culture and Social Responsibility: The Case of Toxic Wastes in a New England Community" Paper Presented at the 1987 meetings of the American Association for the Advancement of Science, Philadelphia.

Nash, J. and M. Kirsch. 1987b. "Polyclorinated Biphenyls and the Electrical Machinery Industry: An Ethnological Study of Community Action and Corporate Responsibility" Social Science and Medicine 23(2): 131-138.

Nash, J. and M. Kirsch. 1988. "The Discourse of Medical Science in the Construction of Consensus Between Corporation and Community." *Medical Anthropology Quarterly* 2(2): 158-71.

Nash, J. 1979. *We Eat the Mines and the Mines Eat Us: Dependency and Exploitation in Bolivian Tin Mines.* New York: Columbia.

Nash, J. 1981. "Ethnographic Aspects of the World Capitalist System" *Annual Reviews in Anthropology.* Palo Alto, Calif.: Stanford University Press.

Nash, J. 1989. *From Tank Town to High Tech.* Albany: State University of New York Press.

Newman, K. 1994."Deindustrialization, Poverty, and Downward Mobility: Toward an Anthropology of Economic Disorder." In S. Forman (ed.), i Ann Arbor: University of Michigan Press.

Newton, E. 1972. *Mother Camp: Female Impersonators in America.* Englewood Clifs, N.J.: Prentice Hall.

Noble, D. 1982. *America by Design.* New York: Knopf.

Noble, D. 1984. "Power and the Power of Ideas." In his *Forces of Production.* Chicago: University of Chicago Press.

North, D. C. 1966. *The Economic Growth of the United States, 1970-1860.* New York: W. W. Norton.

Oakey, R. P. 1984. *High Technology Small Firms: Innovation and Regional Development in Britain and the United States.* New York: St. Martin's.

Offe, C. 1975. "The Theory of the Capitalist State and the Problem of Policy Formation." In L. N. Lindberg et al. (eds.), *Stress and Contradiction in Modern Capitalism: Public Policy and the Theory of the State.* Lexington, Mass.: D. C. Heath and Company.

Parker, R. 1981. "Winning through Inflation." *Mother Jones*, July.

Paul, R. E. 1984. *Divisions of Labour.* New York: Basil Blackwell.

Paul, R. E. 1988. *On Work.* New York: Basil Blackwell.

Peirce, N. R. and C. FD. Steinbach. 1987. *Corrective Capitalism: The Rise of America's Community Development Corporations.* New York: Ford Foundation

Piore, M. J. and C. F. Sabel. 1982. *The Second Industrial Divide.* New York: Basic Books.

Pittsfield Developer's Handbook: How to Locate, Renovate, Construct and Expand. Pittsfield, Mass.: Office of Community and Economic Development.

Pittsfield Economic Revitalization Corporation. 1988. *An Economic Base Study of Pittsfield and Berkshire County.* Pittsfield, Mass.: Author.

Poulantzas, N. 1973. *Political Power and Social Classes.* London: New Left Books.

Poulantzas, N. 1975. *Classes in Contemporary Capitalism.* London: Verso.

Preteceille, E. and J.-P. Terrail. 1985. *Capitalism, Consumption and Needs.* New York: Basil Blackwell.

Prude, J. 1987. "The Social System of Early New England Textile Mills." In H. Gutman and D. H. Bell (eds.), *The New England Working Class and the New Labor History.* Urbana: University of Illinois Press.

Rapp, R. 1987. "Urban Kinship in Contemporary America: Families, Classes and Ideology." In L. Mullings, (ed.), *Cities of the United States.* New York: Columbia University Press.

Redclift, N. and Mingione, E. 1984. *Beyond Employment: Household, Gender and Subsistence.* New York: Basil Blackwell.

Regional Science Research Institute. 1982. *The Berkshire County Economy: Problems and Potentials.* Amherst, Mass.: Author.

Regional Science Research Institute. 1983. *Past Trends in the Economy of Western Massachusetts. Draft Report to the Western Massachusetts Economic Development Conference.* Amherst, Mass.: Author..

Regional Science Research Institute. 1984. *Targeting Measures and Target Industries For Western Massachusetts. Final Report to the Western Massachusetts Economic Development Conference.* Amherst, Mass.: Author.

Rohatyn, F. 1981. "Restructuring America." *New York Review of Books,* February 5.

Rosen, E. 1981. "Job Mobility and Job Loss: A Study of the Effects of Unemployment and Underemployment among Blue-Collar Working Women in New England." Chestnut Hill, Mass.: Social Welfare Research Institute College.

Rosenblum, G. 1973. *Immigrant Workers: Their Impact on American Labor Radicalism.* New York: Basic Books.

Safa, H. 1981. "Runaway Shops and Female Employment: The Search for Cheap Labor." *Signs* 7(2).

Sahlus, M. 1985. *Islands of History.* Chicago. University of Chicago Press.

Schmenner, R. W. 1982. *Making Business Location Decisions.* Englewood Cliffs, N.J.: Prentice Hall.

Schneider, D. 1968. *American Kinship,* Englewood Cliffs, N.J.: Prentice Hall.

Scranton, P. 1984. "Varieties of Paternalism: Industrial Structures and the Social Relations of Production in American Textiles." *American Quarterly* 36: 235-58.

Smith, J. E. A. 1869. *The History of Pittsfield, (Berkshire County) Massachusetts, From the Year 1734 to the Year 1800.* Boston: Lee and Shepard.

Smith, N. 1984. *Uneven Development: Nature, Capital and the Production of Space.* New York: Basil Blackwell.

Snyder, D. and E. Kick. 1979. "Structural Position in the World System and Economic Growth, 1955-1970: A Multiple Network Analysis of Transnational Interaction." *American Journal of Sociology* 84: 1097-1126.

Spindler, G. D. and L. Spindler. 1983. "Anthropologists View American Culture." *Annual Reviews in Anthropology* 12. Stanford:

Spradley, James P. *You Owe Yourself a Drunk: An Ethnography of Urban Nomads.* Boston: Little, Brown.

Stack, Carol. 1974. *All Our Kin.* New York: Harper & Row.

Stanback, T. M. and T. J. Noyelle. 1982. *Cities in Transition: Changing Job Structures in Atlanta, Denver, Buffalo, Phoenix, Columbus (Ohio), Nashville, Charlotte.* Montclair, N.J.: Allanheld Osmun

Stearns, P. W. 1980. "The Effort of Continuity in Working Class Culture." *Journal of Modern History* 52.

Stricken, A. 1979. "Ethnicity and Entrepreneurship in Rural Wisconsin." In S. Greenfield et al. (eds.), *Entrepreneurs in Cultural Context.* Albuquerque: University of New Mexico Press.

Sunkel, O. 1978. "Transnational Capitalism and National Disintegration in Latin America." *Social and Economic Studies* 23(4).

Susser, I. 1982. "Urban Anthropology in the U.S.A." RAIN. (4)

Susser, I. 1982. *Norman Street: Poverty and Politics in an Urban Neighborhood.* New York: Oxford University Press.

Tabb, W. K. and L. Sawers (eds.). 1984. *Marxism and the Metropolis.* New York: Oxford University Press.

Thompson, J. B. 1984. *Studies in the Theory of Ideology.* Berkeley: University of California Press.

Thurow, Lester. 1980. "Reindustrialization and Jobs." *Establishment Economist* 7(6).

Timberlake, M. (ed.). 1985. *Urbanization in the World Economy.* New York: Academic Press.

Timparano, S. 1975. *On Materialism.* London: New Left Books.

Tractenberg, A. 1982. *The Incorporation of America: Culture and Society in the Guilded Age.* New York: Hill and Wang.

Turton, A. 1984. "Limits of Ideological Domination and the Formation of Social Consciousness." In A. Turton and S. Tanable (eds.), *History and Peasant Consciousness in Southeast Asia.* Senri Ethnological Studies 13. Osaka: Japan National Musuem of Ethnology.

Valentine, Bettylou. 1978. *Hustling and Other Hard Work: Life Styles in the Ghetto*. Riverside, N.J.: Free Press.

Vatter, H. O. 1963. *The U.S. Economy in the 1950's*. Chicago: University of Chicago Press.

Wachtel, H. M. 1975. "Class Consciousness and Stratification in the Labor Process." In R. C. Edwards (ed.), *Labor Market Segmentation*. Lexington, Mass.: D.C. Heath.

Wadel, C. 1973. "Now Whose Fault is That? The Struggle for Self-Esteem in the Face of Chronic Unemployment." *Newfoundland Social and Economic Studies* 11.

Walker, R. B. J. 1984. *Culture, Ideology and World Order*. Boulder, Colo.: Westview.

Walt J. and L. H. Massotti (eds.). 1974. *The City in Comparative Perspective: Cross National Research and New Directions in Theory*. New York: Halstead Press.

Warner, William Lloyd and Paul S. Lunt. 1941. *The Social Life of a Modern Community*. New Haven, Conn.: Yale University Press.

Weintraub, S. (ed.). 1986. *Industrial Strategy and Planning in Mexico and the United States*. Boulder, Colo.: Westview Press.

Weisskopf, T. 1979. "Marxian Crisis Theory and the Rate of Profit in the Postwar U.S. Economy." *Cambridge Journal of Economics* 3: 341-78.

Williams, R. 1983a. "An Epoch's End." *New Left Review*: 140 (1).

Williams, R. 1983b. *The Year 2000*. New York: Pantheon.

Wolf, E. R. 1972. *Anthropology*. Englewood Cliffs, N.J.: Prentice Hall.

Wolf, E. R. 1974. "American Anthropologists and American Society." In Dell Hymes (ed.), *Reinventing Anthropology*. New York: Vintage Books.

Wolf, E. R. 1982. *Europe and the People without History*. Berkeley: University of California Press.

Wolf, E. R. 1985. "Ideas and Power." Unpublished manuscript.

Wolfinger, R. 1960. "Reputation and Reality in the Study of Community Power." *American Sociological Review* (3).

Wright, T. 1867. *Some Habits and Customs of the Working Classes*. London: Tinsley Brothers.

Yago, G. 1983. "Urban Policy and National Political Economy." *Urban Affairs Quarterly* 19(1).

Yescombe, E. R. 1968. *Sources of Information on the Rubber, Plastics and Allied Industries*. Oxford: Pergamon Press.

Young, M. and P. Wilmott. 1962. *Family and Kinship in East London*. London: Penquin Books.

Zieger, R. H. 1986. *American Workers, American Unions 1920-1985*. Baltimore: John Hopkins University Press.

Zimbalist, A. (ed.). 1979. *Case Studies on the Labor Process.* New York: Monthly Review.

Zuckerman, M. 1978. "The Social Context of Democracy in Massachusetts." *William and Mary Quarterly.* (4)

Index